THE TRIALS OF SOCRATES

For my friends living and dead

Jeff Alden

Liam Byrne

Kevin Madden

THE TRIALS OF SOCRATES

Six Classic Texts

Edited by C. D. C. Reeve

Hackett Publishing Company, Inc.
Indianapolis/Cambridge

For further information, please address:
Hackett Publishing Company, Inc.
P. O. Box 44937
Indianapolis, Indiana 46244–0937

www.hackettpublishing.com

Cover design by Brian Rak and Abigail Coyle

Interior design by Meera Dash

Library of Congress Cataloging-in-Publication Data
The trials of Socrates : six classic texts / edited by C.D.C. Reeve ; translations by
C.D.C. Reeve, Peter Meineck, and James Doyle.
     p. cm.
    Includes bibliographical references (p.).
    Contents: Euthyphro / Plato — Apology / Plato — Crito / Plato —
Phaedo, 115b1–118a17 / Plato — Clouds / Aristophanes — Socrates' defense
to the jury / Xenophon.
    ISBN 0-87220-590-8 (cloth) — ISBN 0-87220-589-4 (paper)
    1. Socrates. 2. Socrates—Trials, litigation, etc. I. Reeve, C. D. C.,
1948– II. Meineck, Peter, 1967– III. Doyle, James. IV. Plato.
V. Aristophanes. VI. Xenophon.

B312.E5 T75 2002
183'.2—dc21   2001051571

ISBN-13: 978-0-087220-590-1 (cloth)
ISBN-13: 978-0-087220-589-5 (pbk.)

Contents

Acknowledgments

I am grateful to Peter Meineck and James Doyle for allowing me to use and slightly modify their translations of Aristophanes and Xenophon.

My own translations of Plato have benefited from the ever astute comments of John Cooper and from the no less astute ones of an anonymous reader. I owe a huge debt, naturally, to previous translators—especially David Gallop, whose translations would be difficult to equal, let alone surpass, and G. M. A. Grube.

I would like to thank Deborah Wilkes for generous personal and editorial attention; Jay Hullett for being his inimitable self; Meera Dash for seeing the book through production with calm and finesse; Abigail Coyle for helping with the cover design; and, above all, Brian Rak for conceiving of this project, helping bring it to completion, and finding the cover art.

Finally, I am happy to acknowledge support from the Stillman Drake Fund at Reed College and a faculty research award from the University of North Carolina at Chapel Hill.

Note to the Reader

Marginal line numbers and references to them in the notes and introductions refer to the Greek text and are only approximate in the translations themselves.

Introduction

By Socrates' own reckoning he was put on trial twice in Athens: once on the comic stage in Aristophanes' *Clouds*, and once in the King Archon's court by a jury of five hundred or so of his peers (Plato, *Apology* 18a7–b1). Of the second trial—or more accurately of the speech of defense Socrates made at it—we possess two supposed versions. The first is by Plato, who represents himself as present at the trial (*Apology* 38b6). The second is by Xenophon, who wasn't present but reports some of what he was told about it by Hermogenes, who may have been present. Of *Clouds*, we possess not the version to which Socrates refers in the *Apology*, but a later revised version. It is substantially the same play, nonetheless, as we can see from Socrates' own description of it.

Two other Platonic dialogues—*Euthyphro* and *Crito*—are closely related to the *Apology* and illuminate it in different ways. *Euthyphro* takes place as Socrates is on his way to the King Archon's court for a pretrial hearing, and deals with a topic—piety—that is central to the trial itself. *Crito* is set in the prison to which Socrates is confined after he has been found guilty of impiety and sentenced to death, and deals with his reasons for accepting what he believes to be an unjust verdict and sentence. In both dialogues, we see Socrates engaged in the philosophical activities that we only hear described in the *Apology* itself. *Phaedo*, like *Crito*, finds Socrates in prison, now awaiting imminent execution. He speaks about death, about his philosophy, and about the afterlife. Then, with the calm characteristic of him in adversity, and in utter fidelity to his principles, he drinks the hemlock and dies.

In *Clouds* we find a comic parody of a Socrates who is represented as a sophist, subversive of traditional Athenian values—including religious ones.

In Xenophon's *Socrates' Defense to the Jury*, we meet a very different Socrates from either Plato's or Aristophanes'—a man who is wholly orthodox in religious matters, and who provokes the jury into unjustly convicting him of impiety because he wants to avoid the pains of old age.

In this volume, these six related works are brought together for the first time. Those by Plato and Xenophon appear in new, previously unpublished translations, which aim to combine accuracy, accessibility, and readability. In their case, as in the case of *Clouds*, introductions together with ample footnotes provide crucial background information and important cross-references.

Socrates

Socrates was born in Athens in 470/69 B.C.E. and died in 399. He was the son of Phaenarete (a midwife) and Sophroniscus (a stone carver), husband of Xanthippe (and later, or perhaps earlier, of Myrto), and father of three sons, two of whom were still children at the time of his death. In Plato's *Euthyphro* (11b), he traces his ancestry to the mythical sculptor Daedalus, so it may be that he too practiced his father's craft early in life. He served as a hoplite (heavily armored infantryman) in the Athenian army during the Peloponnesian War with Sparta (*Apology* 28e), where he gained attention for his courage, his capacity to tolerate hunger, thirst, and cold, and for powers of concentration that could keep him rooted to the spot for hours on end (Plato, *Symposium* 219e–221d). Since hoplites had to own property and provide their own weapons, Socrates cannot always have been poor. Still, he seems to have been exceptionally frugal in his habits. He often went barefoot, seldom bathed, and wore the same thin cloak winter and summer (Plato, *Symposium* 174a, 219b). In a society that worshipped male beauty, he was noteworthy for his ugliness. He had a snub nose, bulging eyes, thick lips, and a pot belly (Xenophon, *Symposium* 2.18, 5.3–8). Yet such was his personal magnetism that many of the best looking young men followed him around.

In 406 B.C.E., Socrates served on the steering committee (*prytaneis*) of the Athenian Assembly, where he alone voted against an illegal motion to try as a group the generals who had failed to pick up the bodies of the dead after the sea battle at Arginusae (*Apology* 32a–c). Later, at the risk of his own life, he disobeyed the unjust order of the Thirty Tyrants to bring in Leon of Salamis for execution (*Apology* 32c–d).

In 423 B.C.E., Socrates was made the subject of Aristophanes' comedy *Clouds*, where he appears as a generic intellectual who teaches a mixture of amoral sophistic argument and an atheistic mechanistic theory of the cosmos. We may infer that Socrates must have looked enough like other sophists to lend popular credibility to Aristophanes' portrait.

In 399 B.C.E., in any case, Socrates was brought to trial on a charge of corrupting the youth by teaching them not to believe in the gods. He was found guilty—in large part, he claims, because of the prejudice against him fanned by Aristophanes—and condemned by a close vote to death by hemlock poisoning. Central, it seems, to the prosecution's case was one of the most puzzling aspects of Socrates—his *daimonion*, or familiar spiritual voice, which held him back whenever he was about to do something wrong. Though this may, in fact, have been no different from other acceptable forms of religious practice, in someone already suspected of being an atheistic sophist, it no doubt seemed—or could be made to seem—much more sinister and subversive.

Socrates' personal characteristics played—and continue to play—a very significant role in attracting devotees to him. He demonstrates—what every teacher knows—that charisma can be as important as content. If Socrates hadn't had that certain compelling something, who would have listened to what he had to say? As it was, however, many listened. And, since Socrates himself wrote nothing, it is to them that we have to turn for information. The problem is (1) The writings of many of those who knew him—Antisthenes, Phaedo of Elis, Eucleides of Megara, Aristippus of Cyrene, Aeschines of Sphettos—have disappeared or exist only in very fragmentary form. (2) The extant writings of others who knew him—Aristophanes, Plato, and Xenophon—while extensive, present us with very different portraits. (3) Plato's own portrait is—at least—a double one: the Socrates of the early dialogues (*Apology, Charmides, Crito, Euthyphro, Hippias Minor, Hippias Major, Ion, Laches, Lysis, Menexenus*) is thought to be based to some extent on the historical figure (they are often called "Socratic" dialogues for this reason). The Socrates who appears in later dialogues, however, seems to be increasingly a mouthpiece for Plato's own developing doctrines. When we look at Socrates, therefore, we are looking at many potentially different figures. For some were influenced by the historical Socrates, some by portrayals of him only some of which we know, some more by the man and his character, and some more by his specific doctrines.

Nonetheless, a few significant ideas come close to being the common property of these different figures: (1) Knowledge or theory (*logos*) is important for virtue. (2) Virtue is important for happiness. (3) The use of questioning based on *epagōgē* (induction, arguing from parallel cases) is important in regard to the possession of knowledge,

and so of virtue. (4) The sort of self-mastery (*enkrateia*), self-suffi-
ciency (*autarkeia*), and moral toughness (*karteria*) exhibited by Socrates
in regard to pleasures and pains is important for happiness. (5) *Erōs*
and friendship have important roles to play in philosophy—and philosophy, because of (1)–(3), in life. (6) The traditional teachers of virtue—the poets—as well as the alleged embodiments of wisdom—the
politicians—are deficient in various ways revealed by (3).

   These ideas are vague, of course, and so can be understood in various ways. Socrates could hardly have influenced so many different
sorts of people had it been otherwise.

PLATO

Introduction

Plato was born in Athens in 428 B.C.E. and died in 348/7. His father, Ariston, traced his descent to Codrus, the last king of Athens; his mother, Perictione, was related to Solon, architect of the Athenian constitution. While Plato was still a boy, his father died and his mother married Pyrilampes, a friend of the great Athenian statesman Pericles. Plato was thus familiar with Athenian politics from childhood and was expected to take up a political career himself. Horrified by actual political events, however, especially the execution of Socrates in 399 B.C.E., he turned instead to philosophy, thinking that only education in it could rescue humankind from civil war and political upheaval and provide a sound foundation for ethics and politics (*Seventh Letter* 324b–326b).

As Plato represents Socratic philosophy, it consists almost exclusively in questioning people about the conventionally recognized ethical virtues. What is justice?, Socrates asks, or piety? or courage? or wisdom? Moreover, Socrates takes for granted that there are correct answers to these questions—that each virtue is some definite characteristic or form (*eidos, idea*). And though he does not discuss the nature of these forms, or develop any explicit theory of them or our knowledge of them, he does claim that only they can serve as reliable standards for judging whether something is virtuous, and that they can be captured in explicit definitions (*Euthyphro* 6d–e, *Charmides* 158e–159a).

Socrates' interest in definitions of the virtues, Aristotle tells us, resulted from thinking of them as ethical first principles (*Metaphysics* 1078^{b}12–32). That is why, if one does not know them, one cannot know anything else of any consequence about ethics (*Hippias Major* 286c–d, 304d–e; *Laches* 190b–c; *Lysis* 212a, 223b; *Protagoras* 361c; *Republic* 354c). Claiming not to know them himself, Socrates also claims to have little or no other ethical knowledge (*Apology* 20c, 21b). These disclaimers of knowledge are often characterized as false or ironical, but Aristotle took them at face value (*Sophistical Refutations* 183^{b}6–8).

Socrates' characteristic way of questioning people is now called an *elenchus* (from the Greek verb *elegchein*, to examine or refute): Socrates asks what some virtue is; the interlocutor gives a definition he sincerely believes to be correct; Socrates then refutes this definition by showing that it conflicts with other beliefs the interlocutor sincerely holds and is unwilling to abandon (often a consideration of parallel or analogous cases plays an important role in eliciting these beliefs). In the ideal situation, which is never actually portrayed in the Socratic dialogues, this process continues until a satisfactory definition emerges, one that is not inconsistent with other sincerely held beliefs, and so can withstand elenctic scrutiny. Since consistency with false beliefs is no guarantee of truth and untrue definitions are no basis for knowledge, Socrates' use of the elenchus seems to presuppose that some sincerely held beliefs are true.

The definitions Socrates encounters in his elenctic examinations of others prove unsatisfactory. But through these examinations, which are always at the same time self-examinations (*Charmides* 166c–d; *Hippias Major* 298b–c; *Protagoras* 348c–d), he comes to accept some positive theses that have resisted refutation. Among these are the following three famous Socratic "paradoxes": (1) The conventionally distinguished virtues are all identical to wisdom or knowledge (*Charmides* 174b–c; *Euthydemus* 281d–e; *Protagoras* 329b–334c, 349a–361d). (2) This knowledge is necessary and sufficient for happiness or perhaps even identical to it (*Crito* 48b; *Gorgias* 471e). (3) No individuals ever act contrary to what they know or believe to be best, so that weakness of will is impossible (*Protagoras* 352a–358d). Together these three doctrines constitute a very strict kind of ethical intellectualism: they imply that all we need in order to be virtuous and happy is knowledge.

The goal of an elenchus, however, is not just to reach adequate definitions of the virtues, or seemingly paradoxical doctrines about weakness of will and virtue, but *moral education and reform*. For Socrates believes that regular elenctic philosophizing—leading the examined life—makes people happier and more virtuous than anything else by curing them of the hubris of thinking they know when they don't (*Apology* 30a, 36c–e, 38a, 41b–c). Philosophizing is so important for human welfare, indeed, that he is willing to accept execution rather than give it up (*Apology* 29b–d).

EUTHYPHRO

EUTHYPHRO:[1] What's new, Socrates, to make you leave the 2a Lyceum,[2] where you usually spend your time, to spend it here today at the court of the King Archon?[3] Surely, *you* don't have some sort of lawsuit before the King, as I do.

SOCRATES: *Athenians* don't call it a lawsuit, Euthyphro, but an 5 indictment.[4]

EUTHYPHRO: What? Someone has indicted you, apparently, for 2b I'm not going to accuse *you* of indicting someone else!

SOCRATES: No, I certainly haven't.

EUTHYPHRO: But someone else has indicted you?

SOCRATES: Exactly. 5

EUTHYPHRO: Who is he?

SOCRATES: I hardly know the man myself, Euthyphro. He's young and unknown, it seems. But I believe his name's Meletus. He belongs

---

1. Euthyphro was a *mantis*, or prophet (3b9–c5, 3e3), a self-proclaimed authority on Greek religion (4e4–5a2), who takes very literally the stories embodied in its myths (5e3–6b6). If he is the Euthyphro mentioned in Plato's *Cratylus*, he was also interested in language and etymology (396d2–397a2).

2. The Lyceum was one of three great gymnasia outside the city walls of Athens (the others were the Cynosarges and the Academy). Plato's other dialogues also identify it as Socrates' favorite place to hold conversations (*Euthydemus* 271a1; *Symposium* 223d8–12). The Academy was later the site of Plato's own school; the Lyceum that of Aristotle's.

3. The nine archons, chosen annually, were the chief public officials in Athens: one was civilian head of state, one was head of the army (*polemarchos*), and six had judicial roles (*thesmothetai*). The King Archon dealt with important religious matters (such as the indictment against Socrates for impiety) and also with homicide (the subject of Euthyphro's indictment). His court or porch (*stoa*) was in the marketplace (*agora*).

4. A lawsuit (*dikē*) was either private (*dikē idia*) or public (*dikē dēmosia*). A public suit was one thought to affect the community as a whole, and so any free adult male citizen could prosecute it. An indictment (*graphē*) was a specific sort of public suit. Since the indictment Socrates faced was for impiety (*graphē asebeias*), it was subject to a preliminary hearing before the King Archon. If he deemed it to have sufficient merit, it then went to trial in his court before a citizen jury. Socrates is on his way to this preliminary hearing.

to the Pitthean deme[5]—if you recall a Meletus from that deme, with
10   straight hair, not much of a beard, and a slightly hooked nose?

EUTHYPHRO: No, I don't recall him, Socrates. But tell me, what
2c   indictment has he brought against you?

SOCRATES: What indictment? Not a trivial one, it seems to me. I
mean, it's no small thing for a young man to have come to know such
an important matter. You see, according to him, he knows how the
young men are being corrupted, and who's corrupting them. He's
5   probably a wise man, who's seen that my own ignorance is corrupting
his contemporaries, and is coming to accuse me to their mother the
city, so to speak. In fact, he seems to me to be the only one who's
starting up in politics correctly. For it is correct to take care of[6] the
2d   young first, to make them the best possible, just as it's reasonable for a
good farmer to take care of the young plants first, and all the others
afterward. And so Meletus, too, is presumably first weeding out those
3a   of us who corrupt the young shoots, as he claims. Then, after that,
he'll clearly take care of the older people and bring about the greatest
goods, both in number and in quality, for the city. That, at any rate, is
5   the likely outcome of such a start.

EUTHYPHRO: I hope it happens, Socrates, but I'm terribly afraid
the opposite may result. You see, by attempting to do an injustice to
you, it seems to me he's simply starting out by wronging the city at its
very hearth.[7] Tell me, what on earth does he say you're doing that
corrupts the young?

---

5. Meletus is often characterized as a cat's-paw of Anytus—another of Socrates'
accusers (*Apology* 18b2 note). But if he is the Meletus who brought a charge of
impiety against Andocides in 399 B.C.E. (see Lysias, *Against Andocides*), he was not
only one of the people who participated in the arrest of Leon of Salamis under the
Thirty Tyrants—something Socrates refused to do (*Apology* 32c3–e1)—he was
also a religious fanatic, and may well have been the chief instigator of the charges.
It may be, too, that he is the son of the poet of the same name, which would help
explain why he is described as having brought his indictment because he was aggrieved on behalf of the poets Socrates examines (*Apology* 23e5). A deme was a
relatively independent administrative unit rather like a village or township. Athens
consisted of 139 of them.

6. *Epimelēthēnai*: from *epimeleomai*, "to take care of": one of a series of puns on Meletus' name that continues into the *Apology* and *Crito*.

7. The reference is to the communal hearth in the Prytaneum (*Apology* 36d7
note), which was the symbolic center of Athens.

SOCRATES: Strange things, my excellent friend, at any rate on first hearing: he says I'm an inventor of gods. And because I invent new gods, and don't acknowledge the old ones, he's indicted me for the latter's sake, so he says.

3b

EUTHYPHRO: I understand, Socrates. That's no doubt because you say your daimonic sign[8] comes to you on each occasion. So he has written this indictment against you for making innovations in religious matters and comes before the court to slander you, knowing that such things are easy to misrepresent to the majority of people.[9] Why, they even mock *me* as if I were crazy, when I speak in the Assembly[10] on religious matters and predict the future for them! And yet not one of my predictions has failed to come true. But all the same, they envy anyone like ourselves.[11] We mustn't give them a thought, though. Just meet them head on.

5

3c

5

SOCRATES: Yes, my dear Euthyphro, but being mocked is presumably nothing to worry about. Athenians, it seems to me, aren't much concerned if they think someone's clever, so long as he doesn't teach his own wisdom. But if they think he's making other people wise like himself, they get angry, whether out of envy, as you say, or for some other reason.

3d

EUTHYPHRO: As to that, I certainly have no desire to test their attitude toward *me*.

SOCRATES: Don't worry. They probably think you rarely put yourself at other people's disposal, and aren't willing to teach your own wisdom. But I'm afraid they think my love of people makes me tell whatever little I know unreservedly to any man,[12] not only without charging a fee,[13] but even glad to lose money, so long as someone cares

5

---

8. *Daimonion*: See *Apology* 31c7–d4. *The American Heritage Dictionary of the English Language*, 4th ed.: "dai·mon . . . also de·mon or dae·mon . . . *n. Greek Mythology* 1. An inferior deity, such as a deified hero. 2. An attendant spirit; a genius."

9. Five hundred (or 501) of whom will serve on the jury that will eventually try Socrates (*Apology* 36a6 note).

10. The ultimate decision-making power in the Athenian democracy, consisting of all the adult male citizens.

11. That is, people who have the gift of prophecy. Socrates' sign is mantic or prophetic (*Apology* 40a4).

12. See *Apology* 30a3–5.

13. See *Apology* 19d8–20a2, 31a8–c3.

10   to listen to me. So, as I was just saying, if they were going to mock me,
3e   as you say they do you, there'd be nothing unpleasant about their spending time in the law court playing around and laughing.[14] But if they're
going to be serious, the outcome's unclear, except to you prophets.[15]

5   EUTHYPHRO: Well, it will probably come to nothing, Socrates,
and you'll fight your case satisfactorily, as I think I'll fight mine.

SOCRATES: But now, Euthyphro, what *is* this case of yours? Are
you defending or prosecuting?

10   EUTHYPHRO: Prosecuting.

SOCRATES: Whom?

EUTHYPHRO: Someone I'm again thought to be crazy for prose-
4a   cuting.

SOCRATES: What's that? Is your prosecution a wild goose chase?

EUTHYPHRO: The goose is long past chasing: he's quite old.

5   SOCRATES: Who is he?

EUTHYPHRO: My father.

SOCRATES: My good man! Your own *father*?

EUTHYPHRO: Yes, indeed.

SOCRATES: But what's the charge? What's the lawsuit about?

10   EUTHYPHRO: Murder, Socrates.

SOCRATES: In the name of Heracles![16] Well, Euthyphro, I suppose
most people don't know how it can be correct to do this. I mean, I
can't imagine any ordinary person taking that action correctly, but
4b   only someone who's already far advanced in wisdom.

EUTHYPHRO: Yes, by Zeus,[17] Socrates, far advanced indeed.

SOCRATES: Is the man your father killed one of your relatives
then? Of course he must be, mustn't he? You'd hardly be prosecuting
5   him for murder on behalf of a stranger.[18]

---

14. See *Apology* 24c4–8, 27a7–8.

15. See *Apology* 42a3–5.

16. Heracles (Hercules) was a hero of legendary strength. His famous labors—
twelve extraordinarily difficult tasks—are alluded to at *Apology* 22a6–8.

17. The greatest of the Greek gods (5d6–6a1) and king of the Greek pantheon. It
was common, and not blasphemous, to swear by him, and by the other gods.

18. Normally, the close relatives of the victim took responsibility for prosecuting
his murderer.

EUTHYPHRO: It's ridiculous, Socrates, for you to think it makes any difference whether the dead man's a stranger or a relative. It's ridiculous not to see that the sole consideration should be whether the killer killed justly or not. If he did, let him go, if he didn't, prosecute—if, that is to say, the killer shares your own hearth and table.[19] For the pollution's the same if you knowingly associate with such a person and don't cleanse yourself and him by bringing him to justice.

In point of fact, though, the victim was a day laborer[20] of mine, and when we were farming on Naxos,[21] he worked the land there for us. Well, he got drunk, became enraged with one of our household slaves, and cut his throat. So my father tied him hand and foot, threw him in a ditch, and sent a man here to find out from the official interpreter[22] what should be done. In the meantime, he ignored and neglected his captive as a murderer, thinking it mattered nothing if he did die. And that's just what happened: hunger, cold, and being tied up caused his death before the messenger got back from the interpreter.

That's precisely why my father and my other relatives are angry with me: because I'm prosecuting my father for murder on the murderer's behalf, when my father didn't even kill him, so they claim, and when, even if he definitely did kill him, it's wrong—since the dead man was a murderer—to concern yourself with the victim in that case. You see, it's impious, they say, for a son to prosecute his father for murder. Little do they know, Socrates, about the gods' position on the pious and the impious!

SOCRATES: But, in the name of Zeus, Euthyphro, do you think *you* have such exact knowledge about the positions the gods take, and about the pious and the impious, that in the face of these events, you've no fear of acting impiously yourself in bringing your father to trial?

10

4c

5

4d

5

4e

5

---

19. It is because Euthyphro shares hearth and table with his father—and so risks being contaminated by the pollution (*miasma*) thought to adhere to murderers—that he feels especially obliged to prosecute him.

20. A *pelatēs* or *thēs* (15d6) was a free man who worked for his daily hire. He was, therefore, less a member of Euthyphro's household than even a slave would have been.

21. A large island southeast of Athens.

22. *Tou exēgētou*: The *exēgētai* ("interpreters") were three men chosen—perhaps by the Delphic Oracle (*Apology* 21a4 note)—with advising people on difficult legal cases involving bloodshed and other such religious matters.

EUTHYPHRO: I'd be no use at all, Socrates, and Euthyphro would
5a   be no different from the majority of people, if I didn't have exact
knowledge of all such things.

SOCRATES: So, my excellent Euthyphro, the best thing, it seems, is
for me to become your student, and to challenge[23] Meletus on this
5   very point before his case comes to trial, telling him that even in the
past I always considered it of great importance to know about religious matters, and that now, when he says I've done wrong through
improvising and innovating concerning the gods, I've become your
student. Shouldn't I say to him, "Meletus, if you agree that Euthyphro
5b   is wise about the gods, you should also regard me as correctly
acknowledging them and drop the charge. But if you don't agree,
prosecute this teacher of mine rather than me, for corrupting the old
men—myself and his own father, me by his teaching, and his father
5   by admonishment and punishment." If he isn't convinced by me, and
doesn't drop the charge or prosecute you instead of me, shouldn't I
say the same things in court as in my challenge to him?

EUTHYPHRO: Yes, by Zeus, Socrates, and if he tried bringing an
5c   indictment against *me*, I think I'd soon find his weak spots, and the
question in court would very quickly be about him rather than
about me.

SOCRATES: I realize that as well as you do, my dear friend, and
5   that's why I'm eager to become your student. I know that this Meletus, as well as others no doubt, pretends not to notice *you* at all,
whereas he has seen *me* so sharply and so easily that he has indicted
me for impiety.

Now then, in the name of Zeus, tell me what you were just claiming to know so clearly. What sort of thing would you say the holy and
the unholy are, whether in cases of murder or of anything else? Or
5d   isn't the pious itself the same as itself in every action? And conversely,
isn't the impious entirely the opposite of the pious? And whatever's
going to count as impious, isn't it itself similar to itself—doesn't it, as
5   regards impiety, possess one single characteristic?[24]

EUTHYPHRO: Absolutely, Socrates.

---

23. *Prokaleisthai*: Before a case came to trial, either party might challenge the other
in front of witnesses. Refusal of the challenge could then be offered as evidence
in the trial itself.

24. *Mian tina idean*: See 6d9–e6 and note.

SOCRATES: Tell me, then, what do you say the pious and the impious are?

EUTHYPHRO: Very well, I say that what's pious is precisely what I'm doing now: prosecuting those who commit an injustice, such as murder or temple robbery,[25] or those who've done some other such wrong, regardless of whether they're one's father or one's mother or anyone else whatever. Not prosecuting them, on the other hand, is   5e
what's impious.

Why, Socrates, look at the powerful evidence I have that the law[26] requires this—evidence I've already offered to show other people that such actions are right, that one must not let an impious person go, no matter who he may happen to be. You see, those very people   5 acknowledge Zeus as the best and most just of the gods, and yet they agree that he put his own father in fetters because he unjustly swal-   **6a** lowed down his children, and that *he*, in his turn, castrated *his* father because of other similar injustices.[27] Yet they're extremely angry with *me*, because I'm prosecuting *my* father for his injustice. And so they contradict themselves in what they say about the gods and about me.   5

SOCRATES: Could this be the reason, Euthyphro, I face indictment, that when people say such things about the gods, I find them somehow hard to accept? That, it seems, is why some people will say I'm a wrongdoer. But now if you, who know so much about such   10 matters, share these views, it seems that the rest of us must assent to   **6b** them too. I mean, what can we possibly say in reply, when we admit ourselves that we know nothing about them? But tell me, by the god of friendship,[28] do you really believe those stories are true?

EUTHYPHRO: Yes, and still more amazing things, Socrates, that the   5 majority of people don't know.

SOCRATES: And do you believe that there really is war among the gods? And terrible hostilities and battles, and other such things of the

---

25. Since temples housed treasuries of various sorts, temple robbery was the ancient equivalent of bank robbery.

26. Specifically, the religious law on which Euthyphro is a supposed expert.

27. Cronus mutilated his father, Uranus (Sky), by cutting off his genitals when he was copulating with Gaea (Earth). He ate the children he had with his sister Rhea. Aided by her, however, their son Zeus escaped, overthrew Cronus, and fettered him. See Hesiod, *Theogony* 137–210, 456–508.

28. Namely, Zeus.

sort the poets relate, and that the good painters embroider on our sacred
6c objects—I'm thinking particularly of the robe covered with embroideries of such scenes that's carried up to the Acropolis at the Great Panathenaean festival?[29] Are we to say that these are true, Euthyphro?

EUTHYPHRO: Not only those, Socrates, but as I mentioned just
5 now, I will, if you like, tell you lots of other things about religious matters that I'm sure you'll be amazed to hear.

SOCRATES: I wouldn't be surprised. But tell me about them some other time, when we've the leisure. Now, however, try to answer
6d more clearly the very question I asked before. You see, my friend, you didn't teach me adequately earlier when I asked what the pious was, but you told me that what you're now doing is pious, prosecuting your father for murder.

5 EUTHYPHRO: Yes, and what I said was true, Socrates.

SOCRATES: Perhaps. But surely, Euthyphro, there are also many other things you call pious.

EUTHYPHRO: Yes, indeed.

SOCRATES: Do you remember, then, that what I urged you to do wasn't to teach me about one or two of the many pieties,[30] but rather
10 about the form[31] itself, by virtue of which all the pieties are pious? You see, you said, I believe, that it was by virtue of one characteristic[32] that
6e the impieties are impious, and the pieties pious. Or don't you remember?

---

29. The Acropolis, set on the steep rocky hill that dominates Athens, was the central fortress and principal sanctuary of the goddess Athena. It was the site of the Parthenon, as well as of other temples. The Great Panathenaean festival took place every four years and was a more elaborate version of the yearly festival that marked Athena's birthday. At it, her statue in the Parthenon received a new robe embroidered with scenes from the mythical battle of the gods and the giants.

30. *Ta polla hosia*: Socrates could be referring to any or all of the following: (1) things that are particular instances of piety because they have the property of being pious, such as pious actions or pious people; (2) the particular instances of piety present in such actions or people; (3) the particular types of piety of which those instances are instances, such as personal piety.

31. *Eidos.*

32. *Idea: Idea* (characteristic) and *eidos* (form) may be equivalent, or it may be that sameness of characteristic entails sameness of form. In either case, the class of (im)pious things has some real feature in common that makes them (im)pious. And this feature serves as a standard for determining which things really belong in that class and which don't (6e3–6), and explains why this is so (9e4–11b5).

EUTHYPHRO: I do indeed.

SOCRATES: Then teach me what that characteristic itself is, in order that by concentrating on it and using it as a model, I may call pious any action of yours or anyone else's that is such as it, and may deny to be pious whatever isn't such as it.

EUTHYPHRO: If that's what you want, Socrates, that's what I'll tell you.

SOCRATES: That *is* what I want.

EUTHYPHRO: In that case: what's loved by the gods is pious, and what's not loved by the gods is impious.

SOCRATES: Excellent, Euthyphro! You've now given the sort of answer I was looking for. Whether it's true, however, that I don't know. But clearly you'll go on to demonstrate fully that what you say *is* true.

EUTHYPHRO: Yes, indeed.

SOCRATES: Come on, then, let's examine what it is we're saying. A god-loved thing or a god-loved person is pious, whereas a god-hated thing or a god-hated person is impious. And the pious isn't the same as the impious, but its exact opposite. Isn't that what we're saying?[33]

EUTHYPHRO: It is indeed.

SOCRATES: And does it seem to be true?

EUTHYPHRO: It does seem so, Socrates.

SOCRATES: And haven't we also said that the gods quarrel and differ with one another, and that there's mutual hostility among them?

EUTHYPHRO: Indeed, we did say that.

SOCRATES: But what are the issues, my good friend, on which differences produce hostility and anger? Let's examine it this way. If you and I differed about which of two groups was more numerous, would our differences on this issue make us hostile and angry toward one another? Or would we turn to calculation and quickly resolve our differences?

EUTHYPHRO: Of course.

SOCRATES: Again, if we differed about which was larger or smaller, we'd turn to measurement and quickly put a stop to our difference.

EUTHYPHRO: That's right.

---

33. Reading οὐχ οὕτως εἴρηται with Hermann.

SOCRATES: And we'd turn to weighing, I imagine, to settle a dispute about which was heavier or lighter?

EUTHYPHRO: Certainly.

10 SOCRATES: Then what sorts of issues *would* make us angry and hostile toward one another if we disagreed about them and were unable to reach a settlement? Perhaps you can't say just offhand. But examine, while I'm speaking, whether they're issues about the just 7d and unjust, fine and shameful, good and bad. Whenever we become enemies, aren't these the issues on which disagreement and an inability to reach a settlement make enemies of us—both you and I and all 5 other human beings?

EUTHYPHRO: That is the difference, Socrates, and those are the things it has to do with.

SOCRATES: And what about the *gods*, Euthyphro? If indeed they 10 differ, mustn't it be about those same things?

EUTHYPHRO: Absolutely.

SOCRATES: Then, according to your account, my noble Euthy-7e phro, different sets of gods, too, consider different things to be just, or fine or shameful, or good or bad. For if they didn't differ about these, they wouldn't quarrel, would they?

5 EUTHYPHRO: That's right.

SOCRATES: Then are the very things that each group of them regards as fine, good, and just also the ones they love, and are the opposites of these the ones they hate?

EUTHYPHRO: Of course.

SOCRATES: But the very same things, so you say, that some gods 10 consider to be just and others unjust are also the ones that lead them 8a to quarrel and war with one another when they have disputes about them. Isn't that right?

EUTHYPHRO: It is.

SOCRATES: Then the same things, it seems, are both hated and loved by the gods, and so the same things would be both god-hated 5 and god-loved.

EUTHYPHRO: It seems that way.

SOCRATES: So, on your account, Euthyphro, the same things would be both pious and impious.

EUTHYPHRO: Apparently.

SOCRATES: So, you haven't answered my question, my excellent
friend. You see, I wasn't asking you what the self-same thing is that's   10
both pious and impious. But a thing that's god-loved is, it seems, also
god-hated. It follows, Euthyphro, that it wouldn't be at all surprising
if what you're now doing in prosecuting your father was something   8b
pleasing to Zeus but displeasing to Cronus and Uranus, or lovable to
Hephaestus and displeasing to Hera,[34] and similarly for any other gods   5
who may differ from one another on the matter.

EUTHYPHRO: But, Socrates, I think that on this point, at least,
none of the gods do differ—that anyone who has unjustly killed
another should be punished.

SOCRATES: Is that so? Well, what about men, Euthyphro? Have
you never heard them arguing that someone who has killed unjustly   10
or done anything else unjustly should *not* be punished?   8c

EUTHYPHRO: Why yes, they never stop arguing like that, whether
in the law courts or in other places. For people who've committed all
sorts of injustices will do or say anything to escape punishment.[35]   5

SOCRATES: But do they agree, Euthyphro, that they've committed
injustice, and, in spite of agreeing, do they still say that they shouldn't
be punished?

EUTHYPHRO: No, they certainly don't say that.

SOCRATES: So it isn't just anything that they'll do or say. You see, I   10
don't think they'd dare to say or argue that if they act *unjustly*, they
should not be punished. Instead, I think they deny acting unjustly,   8d
don't they?

EUTHYPHRO: That's true, they do.

SOCRATES: So they don't argue that someone who acts unjustly
should not be punished, though they do, perhaps, argue about *who*   5
acted unjustly, *what* his unjust action consisted of, and *when* he did it.

EUTHYPHRO: That's true.

---

34. Hephaestus, the god of fire and of blacksmithing, was armor maker to the
gods. His mother, Hera, the wife and sister of Zeus (4b3 note), threw him off
Olympus because he was lame and deformed. This pleased her, not him. In re-
venge, he made her a throne that held her captive when she sat on it. This pleased
him, not her. Similarly, Cronus cannot have been pleased at being fettered by
Zeus (see 6a3 note).

35. See *Apology* 38d3–39b8.

SOCRATES: Then doesn't the very same thing happen to the gods as well—if indeed they do quarrel about just and unjust actions, as on your account they do, and if one lot says that others have done
10 wrong,[36] and another lot denies it? For surely no one, my excellent friend, whether god or human being, dares to say that one who acts
8e unjustly should not be punished.

EUTHYPHRO: Yes, what you say is true, Socrates, at least the main point.

5   SOCRATES: I think that men and gods who argue, Euthyphro, if indeed gods really do argue, argue instead about *actions*. It's about some action that they differ, some of them saying that it was done justly, others unjustly. Isn't that so?

10   EUTHYPHRO: Of course.

SOCRATES: Come then, my dear Euthyphro, and teach me, too,
9a that I may become wiser. A man committed murder while employed
5   as a day laborer and died as a result of being tied up before the master who tied him up found out from the proper authorities what to do about him. What evidence do you have that all the gods consider this man to have been killed unjustly, and that it's right for a *son* to prosecute and denounce his *father* for murder on behalf of such a man?
9b Come, try to give me a clear proof that all gods undoubtedly consider this action to be right. If you can give me adequate proof of that, I'll never stop praising your wisdom.

5   EUTHYPHRO: But presumably that's no small task, Socrates, though I could of course prove it to you very clearly.

SOCRATES: I understand. You think I'm a slower learner than the jury, since it's clear that you'll prove to *them* that those actions of your father's were unjust and that the gods all hate them.

EUTHYPHRO: I'll prove it to them very clearly, Socrates, provided they'll listen to what I say.

SOCRATES: They'll listen all right, provided you seem to speak
9c well.[37] But a thought occurred to me while you were speaking, and I'm still examining it in my own mind: "Suppose Euthyphro so taught me that I became thoroughly convinced that all the gods do consider a death like that to be unjust. What more would I have

---

36. Reading καὶ οἱ μέν φασιν ἄλλους ἀδικεῖν with Heidel.
37. See *Apology* 17a1–18a6, 35b10–c7, 38d3–e2.

learned from Euthyphro about what the pious and the impious are?   5
That action would indeed be god-hated, so it seems. Yet it became evident just now that the pious and the impious aren't defined by that
fact, since it became evident that what's god-hated is also god-loved.
So I'll let you off on that point,[38] Euthyphro. If you like, let's suppose
that all the gods consider the action unjust, and that they all hate it. Is
that, then, the correction we're now making in the account, that   9d
what *all* the gods hate is impious while what they *all* love is pious, and
that whatever some love and others hate is neither or both? Is that
how you'd now like us to define the pious and the impious?   5

EUTHYPHRO: What's to prevent it, Socrates?

SOCRATES: Nothing on my part, Euthyphro. But you examine
your own view, and whether by assuming it you'll most easily teach
me what you promised.   10

EUTHYPHRO: All right, I'd say that the pious is what all the gods   9e
love, and its opposite, what all the gods hate, is the impious.

SOCRATES: Then aren't we going to examine that in turn, Euthyphro, to see whether what we said is true? Or are we going to let it
alone and accept it from ourselves and from others just as it stands? And   5
if someone merely asserts that something is so, are we going to concede that it's so? Or are we going to examine what the speaker says?

EUTHYPHRO: We're going to examine it. However, I for my part
think that this time what we said *is* true.

SOCRATES: Soon, my good friend, we'll be better able to tell.
Consider the following: is the pious loved by the gods because it's   10a
pious? Or is it pious because it's loved?

EUTHYPHRO: I don't know what you mean, Socrates.

SOCRATES: All right, I'll try to put it more clearly. We speak of a   5
thing's being carried or carrying, and of its being led or leading, and
of being seen or seeing. And you understand that these things are all
different from one another and how they differ?

EUTHYPHRO: I think I understand, at any rate.

---

38. That is, "I won't ask you to show that all the gods hate your father's action,
since even if you could show that, the pious and the impious themselves would
remain undefined." For if some things that are god-hated are also god-loved, then
being god-hated can't be the defining mark of the impious. Socrates goes on to
explain why this is so.

SOCRATES: Then is there also something that's loved, and is it dif-
10 ferent from something that's loving?

EUTHYPHRO: Certainly.

SOCRATES: Then tell me whether the carried thing is a carried
10b thing because it's carried or because of something else.

EUTHYPHRO: No, it's because of that.

SOCRATES: Again, the led thing is so, then, because it's led and the
5 seen thing because it's seen?

EUTHYPHRO: Of course.

SOCRATES: So it's not seen because it's a seen thing; on the contrary, it's a seen thing because it's seen; nor is it because it's a led thing
10 that it's led, rather it's because it's led that it's a led thing; nor is something carried because it's a carried thing, rather it's a carried thing
because it's carried. So is what I mean completely clear, Euthyphro? I
10c mean this: if something's changed in some way or affected in some
way, it's not changed because it's a changed thing; rather, it's a
changed thing because it's changed. Nor is it affected because it's an
affected thing; rather, it's an affected thing because it's affected. Or
5 don't you agree with that?[39]

EUTHYPHRO: I do.

SOCRATES: Then isn't a loved thing, too, either a thing changed or
a thing affected by something?

EUTHYPHRO: Of course.

10 SOCRATES: And so the same holds of it as of our earlier examples:
it's not because it's a loved thing that it's loved by those who love it;
rather it's because it's loved that it's a loved thing?

EUTHYPHRO: Necessarily.

10d SOCRATES: Now what are we saying about the pious, Euthyphro?
On your account, isn't it loved by all the gods?

EUTHYPHRO: Yes.

SOCRATES: So is that because it's pious or because of something
else?

5 EUTHYPHRO: No, it's because it's pious.

---

39. The point is about the dependence of the passive participle—understood as an
adjective—on the passive finite verb. Something becomes an affected thing as a
result of being affected by something that affects it, not the other way around.

SOCRATES: So it's loved because it's pious, not pious because it's loved?

EUTHYPHRO: Apparently.

SOCRATES: On the other hand, what's god-loved is loved—that is to say, god-loved—because the gods love it?[40]   10

EUTHYPHRO: Certainly.

SOCRATES: Then the god-loved is not what's pious, Euthyphro, nor is the pious what's god-loved, as you claim, but one differs from the other.

EUTHYPHRO: How so, Socrates?   10e

SOCRATES: Because we agreed that the pious is loved because it's pious, not pious because it's loved. Didn't we?

EUTHYPHRO: Yes.   5

SOCRATES: The god-loved, on the other hand, is so because it is loved by the gods; it's god-loved by the very fact of being loved. But it's not because it's god-loved that it's being loved.

EUTHYPHRO: That's true.

SOCRATES: But if the god-loved and the pious were really the same thing, my dear Euthyphro, then, if the pious were loved because it's   10
pious, what's god-loved would in turn be loved because it's god-loved; and if what's god-loved were god-loved because it was loved by the   **11a**
gods, the pious would in turn be pious because it was loved by them. But, as it is, you can see that the two are related in the opposite way, as things entirely different from one another. For one of them is lovable because it's loved, whereas the other is loved because it's lovable.   5

And so, Euthyphro, when you're asked what the pious is, it looks as though you don't want to reveal its being to me, but rather to tell me one of its affections—that this happens to the pious, that it's loved by all the gods. What explains it's being loved, however, you still haven't said.[41] So please don't keep it hidden from me, but rather say   11b

---

40. Reading καὶ θεοφιλὲς ⟨τὸ θεοφιλές⟩ with Bast and S. Marc Cohen, "Socrates on the Definition of Piety: *Euthyphro* 10A–11B," *Journal of the History of Philosophy* 9 (1971): n. 19.

41. If I ask you what F is, you answer correctly if you give me a standard (the form of F) that (a) enables me reliably to determine which things are F, and (b) explains why they are F (5d3–4 note)—this is F's being or essence (*ousia*). If you only tell me some affection (*pathos*) F has, while you tell me what F is *like*, you don't tell me what it *is* in the requisite sense.

again from the beginning what it is that explains the pious' being loved by the gods or having some other affection—for we won't disagree about which ones it has. Summon up your enthusiasm, then, 5   and tell me what the pious and the impious are.

EUTHYPHRO: But Socrates, *I* have no way of telling you what I have in mind. For whatever proposals we put forward keep somehow moving around and won't stay put.

SOCRATES: Your proposals, Euthyphro, seem to be the work of my
11c ancestor, Daedalus! Indeed, if I were to state them and put them forward myself, you might perhaps make a joke of me, and say that it's because of my kinship with him that my works of art in words run away and won't stay put.[42] But, as it is, the proposals are your own. So 5   you need a different joke, since it's for *you* that they won't stay put, as you can see yourself.

EUTHYPHRO: But it seems to me, Socrates, that pretty much the same joke does apply in the case of our definitions. You see, *I'm* not the one who makes them move around and not stay put. Rather, *you*
11d seem to me to be the Daedalus, since as far as I'm concerned they would have stayed put.

SOCRATES: Then, my friend, it looks as though I've grown cleverer in my area of expertise[43] than my venerated ancestor, in that he 5   made only his own works not stay put, whereas I do this to my own, it seems, and also to other people's. And the most subtle thing about my area of expertise is that I'm wise in it without wanting to be. You see, I'd prefer to have accounts stay put and be immovably established for me than to acquire the wealth of Tantalus[44] and the wisdom of

---

42. Daedalus was a legendary sculptor of great skill. His statues were so lifelike that they moved around by themselves just like living things. Socrates' father, Sophroniscus, is alleged to have been a sculptor or stone carver (Diogenes Laertius II.18), and some of the statues on the Acropolis may have been attributed to Socrates himself (Pausanias I.22).

43. *Technē*: The *technai* include crafts, such as carpentry and shoemaking; fine arts, such as painting and sculpting; arts or sciences, such as medicine and geometry; and more generally any acknowledged area of expertise.

44. Tantalus, son of Zeus, was a legendary king proverbial for his wealth, who enjoyed the privilege of dining with the gods. He killed and cooked his son, Pelops, and mixed pieces of his flesh in with their food to see if they could detect it. He was punished in Hades by being "tantalized"—any food or water he reached for always eluded his grasp.

Daedalus combined.[45] But enough of this. Since you seem to me to   11e
be getting sated, I'll do my best to help you teach me about the
pious—and don't you give up before you do. See whether you don't
think that the pious as a whole must be just.   5

EUTHYPHRO: Yes, I do.

SOCRATES: Then is the just as a whole also pious? Or while the
pious as a whole is just, is the just as a whole not pious, but part of it   **12a**
pious and part of it something else?

EUTHYPHRO: I don't follow what you're saying, Socrates.

SOCRATES: And yet you're as much younger as wiser than I. But as
I say, your wealth of wisdom has weakened you. Well, pull yourself
together, my dear fellow. What I'm saying isn't hard to understand.
You see, what I'm saying is just the opposite of what the poet said,
who wrote:

> *With Zeus the maker, who caused all these things to come about,*
> *You will not quarrel, since where there's dread there's shame too.*[46]   12b

I disagree with this poet. Shall I tell you where?

EUTHYPHRO: Of course.

SOCRATES: It doesn't seem to me that "where there's dread there's
shame too." For many people seem to me to dread disease and poverty and many other things of that sort, but though they dread them,   5
they feel no shame at what they dread. Or don't you agree?

EUTHYPHRO: Of course.

SOCRATES: But where there's shame, there is also dread. For if
anyone feels shame at a certain action—if he's ashamed of it—doesn't
he fear, doesn't he dread, a reputation for wickedness at the same   10
time?   12c

EUTHYPHRO: He certainly does dread it.

SOCRATES: Then it isn't right to say that "where there's dread,
there's shame too." But where there's shame there's also dread, even
though shame isn't found everywhere there's dread. You see, dread is

---

45. Because knowing what virtue is is necessary and sufficient for being virtuous
(presupposed at *Apology* 29d2–30a2) and being virtuous is necessary and sufficient
for being happy (*Crito* 48b8 and note).

46. Author unknown.

5 broader than shame, I think. For shame is a part of fear, just as odd is of number. Hence where there's a number, there isn't something odd too, but where there's something odd there is also a number. Do you follow me now at least?

EUTHYPHRO: Of course.

SOCRATES: Well, that's the sort of thing I was asking just now: whenever there's something just, is there also something pious? Or is
12d something just whenever it's pious, but not pious whenever it's just, because the pious is part of the just? Is that what we're to say, or do you disagree?

EUTHYPHRO: No, let's say that, since it seems to me you're right.

SOCRATES: Then consider the next point. If the pious is a part of
5 what's just, we must, it seems, find out what part of the just the pious is. Now if you asked me about one of the things we just mentioned, for example, which part of number is the even—that is to say, what sort of number it is—I'd say that it's any number not indivisible by
10 two, but divisible by it. Or don't you agree?

EUTHYPHRO: Yes, I do.

SOCRATES: Then you try to teach me in the same fashion what
12e part of the just is pious. Then we can tell Meletus not to treat us unjustly any longer or indict us for impiety, since I've now been suffi-ciently instructed by you about what things are holy or pious and
5 what aren't.

EUTHYPHRO: Well then, it seems to me, Socrates, that the part of the just that's holy or pious is the one concerned with tending to the gods, while the remaining part of the just is concerned with tending to human beings.

SOCRATES: You seem to me to have put that very well, Euthyphro.
13a But I'm still lacking one small piece of information. You see, I don't yet understand this tending you're talking about. You surely don't mean that in just the way that there's tending to other things, there's tending to the gods too. We do speak this way, don't we? We say, for example, that not everyone knows how to tend to horses, but only
5 horse trainers.[47] Isn't that right?

EUTHYPHRO: Of course.

SOCRATES: Because horse training is expertise in tending to horses?

---

47. See *Apology* 25a13–b6.

EUTHYPHRO: Yes.

SOCRATES: Nor does everyone know how to tend to dogs, but only dog trainers. 10

EUTHYPHRO: That's right.

SOCRATES: Because dog training is expertise in tending to dogs.

EUTHYPHRO: Yes. 13b

SOCRATES: And cattle breeding is expertise in tending to cattle.

EUTHYPHRO: Of course.

SOCRATES: Well, but piety or holiness is tending to the gods, Euthyphro? That's what you're saying? 5

EUTHYPHRO: It is.

SOCRATES: But doesn't all tending accomplish the same end? I mean something like some good or benefit for what's being tended to—as you see that horses tended to by horse trainers are benefited and made better. Or don't you agree that they are? 10

EUTHYPHRO: Yes, I do.

SOCRATES: And so dogs, of course, are benefited by dog training and cattle by cattle breeding, and similarly for all the others. Or do 13c you think that tending aims to harm what's being tended?

EUTHYPHRO: No, by Zeus, I don't.

SOCRATES: Rather, it aims to benefit it?

EUTHYPHRO: Certainly. 5

SOCRATES: Then if piety is tending to the gods, does it benefit the gods and make the gods better? Would you concede that whenever you do something pious, you're making some god better?

EUTHYPHRO: No, by Zeus, I wouldn't. 10

SOCRATES: No, I didn't think that that was what you meant, Euthyphro—far from it. But it is why I asked what you did mean by tending to the gods, because I didn't think you meant that sort of 13d tending.

EUTHYPHRO: And you were right, Socrates, since that's not the sort I meant.

SOCRATES: All right. But then what sort of tending to the gods would the pious be? 5

EUTHYPHRO: The very sort of tending, Socrates, that slaves provide to their masters.

SOCRATES: I understand. Then it would seem to be some sort of service to the gods.

EUTHYPHRO: It is indeed.

SOCRATES: Now could you tell me about service to doctors? 10 What result does that service—insofar as it is service—aim to produce? Don't you think it aims at health?

EUTHYPHRO: I do.

13e   SOCRATES: What about service to shipbuilders? What result does the service aim to produce?

EUTHYPHRO: Clearly, Socrates, its aim is a ship.

SOCRATES: And in the case of service to builders, I suppose, the aim is a house?

5   EUTHYPHRO: Yes.

SOCRATES: Then tell me, my good friend, at what result does service to the gods aim? Clearly, you know, since you say you've a finer knowledge of religious matters than any other human being.[48]

10   EUTHYPHRO: Yes, and what I say is true, Socrates.

SOCRATES: Then tell me, in the name of Zeus, what is that supremely fine result that the gods produce by using our services?

EUTHYPHRO: They produce many fine ones, Socrates.

14a   SOCRATES: So too do generals, my friend. Nonetheless, you could easily tell me the main one, which is to produce victory in war, is it not?

EUTHYPHRO: Certainly.

5   SOCRATES: And farmers, too, I think, produce many fine results. Nonetheless, the main one is to produce food from the earth.

EUTHYPHRO: Of course.

SOCRATES: What, then, about the many fine results that the gods 10 produce? Which is the main one they produce?

EUTHYPHRO: I told you a moment ago, Socrates, that it's a pretty 14b difficult task to learn the exact truth about all these matters. But to put it simply: if a person knows how to do and say the things that are pleasing to the gods in prayer and sacrifice—those are the ones that are pious. And actions like them preserve both the private welfare of households and the common welfare of the city, whereas those that

---

48. See *Apology* 24d3–4.

are the opposite of pleasing are unholy, and they, of course, overturn   5
and destroy everything.

SOCRATES: If you'd wanted to, Euthyphro, you could have put the
main point I asked about much more briefly. But you're not eager to
teach me—that's clear. You see, when you were just now on the point   14c
of answering you turned away. If you had given the answer, I'd
already have been adequately instructed by you about piety. But as it
is, the questioner must follow the one being questioned wherever he
leads.[49] Once again, then, what are you saying that the pious, or piety,
is? Didn't you say that it was some sort of knowledge of sacrificing   5
and praying?

EUTHYPHRO: Yes, I did.

SOCRATES: And sacrificing is giving to the gods, and praying is
asking from them?

EUTHYPHRO: Yes, indeed, Socrates.   10

SOCRATES: So, on that account, piety would be knowing how to
ask from the gods and how to give to them.   14d

EUTHYPHRO: You've grasped my meaning perfectly, Socrates.

SOCRATES: Yes, my friend, that's because I really desire your wisdom and apply my mind to it, so that what you say won't fall on bar-
ren ground. But tell me, what is this service to the gods? You say it's   5
asking for things from them and giving things to them?

EUTHYPHRO: I do.

SOCRATES: Well then, wouldn't asking in the right way consist of
asking for the things we need from them?   10

EUTHYPHRO: What else could it be?

SOCRATES: And, conversely, giving in the right way would consist
of giving them, in turn, the things they need from us? For surely giv-   14e
ing someone what he didn't at all need isn't something that an expert
in the art of giving would do.

EUTHYPHRO: That's true, Socrates.   5

SOCRATES: Then piety, Euthyphro, would be a sort of expertise in
mutual trading between gods and men.

---

49. Reading τὸν ἐρωτῶντα τῷ ἐρωτωμένῳ . . . ὑπάγῃ with the revised OCT.
Burnet prints τὸν ἐρῶντα τῷ ἐρωμένῳ . . . ὑπάγῃ: "the lover must follow the beloved."

EUTHYPHRO: Yes, trading, if that's what you prefer to call it.

SOCRATES: I don't prefer anything, if it isn't true.[50] But tell me, what benefit do the gods get from the gifts they receive from us? I mean, what they give is clear to everyone, since we possess nothing good that they don't give us. But how are they benefited by what they receive from us? Or do we get so much the better of them[51] in the trade that we receive all our good things from them while they receive nothing from us?

EUTHYPHRO: But Socrates, do you really think gods are benefited by what they receive from us?

SOCRATES: If not, Euthyphro, what could those gifts of ours to gods possibly be?

EUTHYPHRO: What else do you think but honor and reverence and—as I said just now—what's pleasing to them.[52]

SOCRATES: So is the pious pleasing to the gods, Euthyphro, but not beneficial to them or loved by them?

EUTHYPHRO: No, I think that it's in fact the most loved of all.

SOCRATES: So, once again, it seems, the pious is what's loved by the gods.

EUTHYPHRO: Absolutely.

SOCRATES: Well, if you say that, can you wonder that your accounts seem not to stay put but to move around? And will you accuse me of being the Daedalus who makes them move, when you yourself are far more expert than Daedalus in the art of making them move in a circle? Or don't you see that our account has circled back again to the same place? For surely you remember that earlier we discovered the pious and the god-loved are not the same, but different from one another. Or don't you remember that?

EUTHYPHRO: Yes, I do.

SOCRATES: Then don't you realize that you're now saying the pious is what the gods love? And that's the same, isn't it, as what's god-loved? Or is that not so?

EUTHYPHRO: Of course, it is.

---

50. See *Crito* 46b4–47a5.

51. *Pleonektoumen*: to get the better of, typically in an unjust way.

52. See 14b2–7.

SOCRATES: Then either we weren't right to agree before, or, if we were right, our present suggestion is wrong.

EUTHYPHRO: So it seems.   10

SOCRATES: So we must examine again from the beginning what the pious is, since I won't willingly give up until I learn this. Don't scorn me, but apply your mind to the matter in as many ways and as   15d fully as you can, and then tell me the truth—for you must know it, if indeed any human being does,[53] and, like Proteus,[54] you mustn't be let go until you tell it. For if you didn't know with full clarity what the pious and the impious are, you'd never have ventured to prosecute your old father for murder on behalf of a day laborer. On the contrary, you wouldn't have risked acting wrongly because you'd have been afraid before the gods and ashamed before men. As things stand, however, I well know that you think you have fully clear knowledge of what's pious and what isn't.[55] So tell me what you think it is, my excellent Euthyphro, and don't conceal it.

EUTHYPHRO: Some other time, Socrates. You see, I'm in a hurry to get somewhere, and it's time for me to be off.

SOCRATES: What a way to treat me, my friend! Going off like that and dashing the high hopes I had that I'd learn from you what things are pious and what aren't. Then I'd escape Meletus' indictment by showing him that Euthyphro had now made me wise in religious matters, and ignorance would no longer cause me to improvise and innovate about them.[56] What's more, I'd live a better way for the rest of my life.

---

53. See *Apology* 23a5–b4.

54. Proteus, the Old Man of the Sea, was a god who could change himself into any shape he wished. In this way, he avoided being captured, until his daughter, Eidothea, revealed the secret: keep tight hold of him, no matter what he changes into. See Homer, *Odyssey* IV.351–569.

55. See *Apology* 21e6–24b2.

56. See *Apology* 25c5–26a8.

The Apology[1] of Socrates

17a   I don't know, men of Athens,[2] how you were affected by my accusers. As for me, I was almost carried away by them, they spoke so persuasively. And yet almost nothing they said is true. Among their many
5   falsehoods, however, one especially amazed me: that you must[3] be careful not to be deceived by me, since I'm a dangerously clever
17b   speaker. That they aren't ashamed at being immediately refuted by the facts, once it becomes apparent that I'm not a clever speaker at all, that seems to me most shameless of them. Unless, of course, the one they call "clever" is the one who tells the truth. If that's what they
5   mean, I'd agree that I'm an orator—although not one of their sort. No, indeed. Rather, just as I claimed, they have said little or nothing true, whereas from me you'll hear the whole truth. But not, by Zeus,[4] men of Athens, expressed in elegant language like theirs,
17c   arranged in fine words and phrases. Instead, what you hear will be spoken extemporaneously in whatever words come to mind, and let none of you expect me to do otherwise—for I put my trust in the justice of what I say. After all, it wouldn't be appropriate at my age,
5   gentlemen, to come before you speaking in polished, artificial language like a young man.[5]

Indeed, men of Athens, this I positively entreat of you: if you hear me making my defense using the same sort of language[6] that I'm accustomed to use both in the marketplace next to the bankers' tables—where many of you have heard me—and also in other places,
10   please don't be surprised or create an uproar on that account. For the

---

1. *Apologia*: not an apology in our sense of the term, in which error or wrongdoing is admitted, but a defense against an accusation or charge.

2. Socrates reserves the more common formula "gentlemen of the jury" (*ō andres dikastai*) for those who, because they vote for his acquittal, merit the name "juror." See 40a2 and *Gorgias* 522c1–2.

3. Reading χρή with some mss.

4. See *Euthyphro* 4b3 note.

5. A reference to Socrates' accuser Meletus (19b1 note), who is characterized as "young and unknown" (*Euthyphro* 2b8–9) and as guilty of "youthful rashness" (26e9 below).

6. At 27a10–b2 Socrates makes clear he is referring especially to his characteristic style of argumentative questioning and examining—the so-called elenchus.

fact is that this is the first time I've appeared before a law court, 17d
although I'm seventy years old. So the language of this place is totally
foreign to me. Now, if I were really a foreigner, you'd certainly for-
give me if I spoke in the accents and manner in which I'd been raised.   5
So now, too, I'm asking you, justly it seems to me, to overlook my   18a
manner of speaking (maybe it will be less good, maybe it will be better), but consider and apply your mind to this alone, whether I say
what's just or not. For that's the virtue or excellence[7] of a juror,[8] just
as the orator's lies in telling the truth.   5

The first thing justice demands, then, men of Athens, is that I
defend myself from the first false accusations made against me and
from my first accusers, and then from the later accusations and the
later accusers. You see, many people have been accusing me in front
of you for very many years now—and nothing they say is true. And I   18b
fear them more than Anytus[9] and the rest, though the latter are dangerous as well. But the earlier ones, gentlemen, are more dangerous.
They got hold of most of you from childhood and persuaded you   5
with their accusations against me—accusations no more true than
the current ones. They say there's a man called Socrates, a "wise"
man, a thinker about things in the heavens, an investigator of all

---

7. The virtue or excellence (*aretē*) of a knife or a man is that state or property of it
that makes it a good knife or a good man (e.g., *Republic* 353d9–354a2). The *aretē*
of a knife includes having a sharp blade; the *aretē* of a man includes being intelligent, well born, just, or courageous. *Aretē* is therefore broader than our notion of
moral virtue: it applies to things (such as knives) that are not moral agents, and to
aspects of moral agents (such as intelligence or family status) that are not normally
considered to be moral aspects of them. For these reasons it is sometimes more
appropriate to render *aretē* as "excellence." But "virtue" remains the best overall
translation.

8. A member of an Athenian jury (a *dikastēs*) combined the responsibilities divided
between judge and jury in our legal system. Hence *dikastēs* is sometimes translated
as "judge" and sometimes (as in the present translation) as "juror."

9. Anytus was a democratic leader who helped restore democracy to Athens in
403 B.C.E. after the overthrow of the Thirty Tyrants (32c4 note), under whom he
had lost most of his wealth. As a general in the Athenian army he faced indictment,
but allegedly "bribed the jury and was acquitted" (Aristotle, *Constitution of Athens*
27.5). There is evidence that he believed Socrates was responsible for the ruin of
his son (Xenophon, *Socrates' Defense* 29–31), and that he was passionately opposed
to the sophists (Plato, *Meno* 89e6–92c5).

things below the earth, and someone who makes the weaker argu-
18c   ment the stronger.[10] Those who've spread this rumor, men of Athens, are my dangerous accusers, since the people who hear them
believe that those who investigate such things do not acknowledge
the gods either.[11] Moreover, those accusers are numerous and have
5   been accusing me for a long time now. Besides, they also spoke to
you at that age when you would most readily believe them, when
some of you were children or young boys. Thus they simply won
their case by default, as there was no defense. But what's most
unreasonable in all this is that I can't discover even their names and
tell them to you—unless one of them happens to be a comic play-
18d   wright.[12] In any case, the ones who used malicious slander to persuade you—as well as those who persuaded others after having been
persuaded themselves—all of these are impossible to deal with. One
cannot bring any of them here to court or cross-examine them. One
5   must literally fight with shadows to defend oneself and cross-examine
with no one to respond.

So you too, then, should allow, as I claimed, that there are two
groups of accusers: those who accused me just now and the older
ones I've been discussing. Moreover, you should consider it proper
18e   for me to defend myself against the latter first, since you've heard
them accusing me earlier, and at much greater length, than these
recent ones here.

5   All right. I must defend myself, then, men of Athens, and try to
19a   take away in this brief time[13] prejudices you acquired such a long time
ago. Certainly, that's the outcome I'd wish for—if it's in any way better for you and for me—and I'd like to succeed in my defense.[14] But I
5   think it's a difficult task, and I am not at all unaware of its nature. Let
it turn out, though, in whatever way pleases the god. I have to obey
the law and defend myself.

Let's examine, then, from the beginning, what the charge is
from which the slander against me arose—the very one on which

---

10. See 19b4–21c3 and notes.

11. Atheism, therefore, is the common thread between the ancient accusations
and the formal indictment Socrates now faces. See 26b2–c8, *Laws* 966d4–967d2.

12. The great Athenian dramatist Aristophanes (c. 450–385 B.C.E.), whose play
Clouds, referred to below, presents a hostile portrait of Socrates.

13. There was a time limit on the speeches in an Athenian trial (see 37a8–b2).

14. Compare Xenophon, *Socrates' Defense* 1.

Meletus[15] relied when he wrote the present indictment[16] of me.   19b
Well, then, what exactly did the slanderers say to slander me? Just
as if they were real accusers their affidavit must be read. It's something like this:

> Socrates commits injustice and is a busybody, in that he investigates
> the things beneath the earth and in the heavens,[17] makes the weaker   5
> argument the stronger,[18] and teaches these things to others.   19c

Indeed, you saw these charges expressed yourselves in Aristophanes'
comedy.[19] There, some fellow named Socrates swings around claiming he's walking on air and talking a lot of other nonsense on subjects
that I know neither a lot nor a little but nothing at all about.[20] Not   5
that I mean to disparage this knowledge, if anyone's wise in such subjects—I don't want to have to defend myself against more of Meletus'
lawsuits!—but I, men of Athens, take no part in them.[21] I call on the
majority of you as witnesses to this, and I appeal to you to make it   19d
perfectly plain to one another—those of you who've heard me con-
versing (as many of you have). Tell one another, then, whether any of
you has ever heard me discussing such subjects, either briefly or at
length, and from this you'll realize that the other things commonly   5
said about me are of the same baseless character.

---

15. See *Euthyphro* 2b10 note.

16. The indictment—a *graphē asebeias*—was for impiety.

17. Compare *Clouds* 228. Socrates responds to this slander at 19c6–d7.

18. Compare *Clouds* 112–118. The phrase is a quotation from Protagoras of Ab-
dera, the famous fifth-century sophist (Aristotle, *Rhetoric* 1402ª23 = DK 80B6b).
See 19e4 and note. Socrates responds to this charge at 19d8–20c3.

19. The version of *Clouds* referred to here, which is earlier than the revised version we possess, was first staged in 423 B.C.E..

20. *Clouds* 218 ff.

21. At *Phaedo* 96a6–99d2, Socrates claims that when he was young he was "re-
markably keen on the kind of wisdom known as natural science." Instead of leading him to develop physical theories of his own, however, that interest led him to
agnosticism: "I finally judged myself to have absolutely no gift for this kind of inquiry. I'll tell you a good enough sign of this: there had been things that I previously did know for sure, at least I and others thought we knew them; yet I was
then so utterly blinded by this kind of inquiry that I unlearned even those things
I formerly supposed I knew" (96c1–6). Eventually, he abandoned the study of nature altogether (99d4–5).

In any case, none of them is true. And if you've heard from anyone that I undertake to educate people and charge fees,[22] that's not true either. Although, it also seems to me to be a fine thing if anyone's able to educate people in the way Gorgias of Leontini does, and Prodicus of Ceos, and Hippias of Elis.[23] For each of them, gentlemen, can enter any city and persuade the young—who may associate with any of their own fellow citizens they want to free of charge—to abandon those associations, and associate with them instead, pay them a fee, and be grateful to them besides.

Since we're on that topic, I heard that there's another wise gentleman here at present, from Paros. For I happened to run into a man who has spent more money on sophists than everyone else put together—Callias, the son of Hipponicus.[24] So I questioned him, since he has two sons himself.

"Callias," I said, "if your two sons had been born colts or calves, we could engage and pay a knowledgeable supervisor—one of those expert horse breeders or farmers—who could turn them into fine and good examples of their proper virtue or excellence. But now, seeing that they're human beings, whom do you have in mind to engage as a supervisor? Who is it that has the knowledge of *this* virtue, the virtue of human beings and of citizens? I assume you've

---

22. *Clouds* 98, 245 f., 1146 ff.

23. All three, like Evenus of Paros mentioned below, were sophists—itinerant professors who charged sometimes substantial fees for popular lectures and specialized instruction in a wide variety of fields, including natural science, rhetoric, grammar, ethics, and politics. Sophists did not constitute a single school or movement, however, and were neither doctrinally nor organizationally united. Gorgias of Leontini in Sicily (c. 480–376) was primarily a teacher of rhetoric, noted for his distinctive style. He is the author of the *Defense of Palamedes*, parts of which bear a striking resemblance to the *Apology* and may have either influenced or been influenced by it. Plato named a dialogue critical of rhetoric after him. Prodicus of Ceos, about whom little is known, was also a fifth-century teacher of rhetoric, with an interest in fine distinctions of meaning (*Protagoras* 337a1–c4) and the correctness of names (*Cratylus* 384a8–c2). Hippias of Elis, like Prodicus a contemporary of Socrates, claimed expertise in astronomy, physics, grammar, poetry, and other subjects. Two Platonic dialogues are named after him; he also appears in *Protagoras* (315b9–c7, 337c6–338b1).

24. Callias was one of the richest men in Greece and a patron of the sophists. Both Plato's *Protagoras* and Xenophon's *Symposium* are set in his house.

investigated the matter, because you have two sons. Is there such a   5
person," I asked, "or not?"

"Certainly," he replied.

"Who is he?" I said.

"His name's Evenus, Socrates," he replied, "from Paros. He charges
five minas."[25]

I thought Evenus blessedly happy if he truly did possess that expertise[26] and taught it for so modest a fee. I, at any rate, would pride   20c
myself and give myself airs if I had knowledge of those things. But in
fact, men of Athens, I don't know them.

Now perhaps one of you will interject: "But Socrates, what, then,
is *your* occupation? What has given rise to these slanders against you?   5
Surely if you weren't in fact occupied with something out of the
ordinary, if you weren't doing something different from most people,
all this rumor and talk wouldn't have arisen. Tell us, then, what it is,
so that we don't judge you hastily." These are fair questions, I think,   20d
for the speaker to ask, and I'll try to show you just what it is that has
brought me this slanderous reputation. Listen, then. Perhaps, some of
you will think I'm joking. But you may be sure that I'll be telling you   5
the whole truth.

You see, men of Athens, I've acquired this reputation because of
nothing other than a sort of wisdom. What sort of wisdom, you ask,
is that? The very sort, perhaps, that is *human* wisdom. For it may just
be that I really do have that sort of wisdom, whereas the people I
mentioned just now may, perhaps, be wise because they possess *super-
human* wisdom. I don't know what else to call it, since I myself cer-   20e
tainly don't possess that knowledge, and whoever says I do is lying
and speaking in order to slander me.

Please don't create an uproar, men of Athens, even if you think I'm
somehow making grand claims. You see, I'm not the author of the
story I'm about to tell, though I'll refer you to a reliable source. In   5
fact, as a witness to the existence of my wisdom—if indeed it is a sort
of wisdom—and to its nature, I'll present the god at Delphi to you.[27]

---

25. Evenus is described as a poet (*Phaedo* 60c8–e1) and as an orator (*Phaedrus*
267a1–5). A few fragments of his elegies survive. A drachma was a day's pay for
someone engaged in public works; a mina was a hundred silver drachmas.

26. *Technē*: See *Euthyphro* 11d4 note.

27. Apollo—god of, among other things, healing, prophecy, purification, care for
young citizens, music, poetry.

You remember Chaerephon, no doubt.[28] He was a friend of mine
21a from youth and also a friend of your party, who shared your recent
exile and restoration.[29] You remember, then, what sort of man
Chaerephon was, how intense he was in whatever he set out to do.
Well, on one occasion in particular he went to Delphi and dared to
5 ask the oracle[30]—as I said, please don't create an uproar, gentlemen—
he asked, exactly as I'm telling you, whether anyone was wiser than
myself. The Pythia[31] drew forth the response that no one is wiser. His
brother here will testify to you about it, since Chaerephon himself is
dead.[32]

Please consider my purpose in telling you this, since I'm about to
21b explain to you where the slander against me has come from. You see,
when I heard these things, I thought to myself as follows: "What can

---

28. A long-time companion of Socrates. He makes brief appearances in *Charmides*
and *Gorgias*, and in *Clouds* 102–104, 144–147, 156 ff., 500–504, 831.

29. Members of the democratic party left Athens when the Thirty Tyrants (see
32c4 note) came to power in 404 B.C.E. They returned to power when the tyrants
were overthrown in 403.

30. The Delphic Oracle was one of the most famous in antiquity. There were
two methods of consulting it. One, involving the sacrifice of sheep and goats,
was quite expensive but resulted in a written response. The other—the so-called
method of the two beans—was substantially cheaper but resulted only in a response by lot. Since Chaerephon was notoriously poor, it seems probable that he
consulted the oracle by the latter method (something also suggested by Socrates'
characterization of the priestess as *drawing forth* the response at 21a6–7). The in-
scriptions on the walls of the temple well convey the spirit the oracle stood for:
know thyself; nothing in excess; observe the limit; hate hubris; bow before the
divine; glory not in strength. There is no unambiguous record of the oracle ever
having praised anyone for what we would think of as his significant or noteworthy positive achievements or abilities. On the other hand, there are many stories
of the following kind. Someone powerful, grand, famous for his wisdom, or in
some other way noteworthy for his accomplishments asks the oracle to say who
is wisest, most pious, happiest, or what have you, expecting that he himself will
be named. But the oracle names some unknown person living in humble and
quiet obscurity. What we know about the oracle, then, makes it very unlikely
that it was praising Socrates for his positive contributions to wisdom and very
likely that it was using him—as he himself comes to believe it was (23a5–b4)—
as an example of someone who was wise because he made no hubristic claims to
wisdom.

31. The priestess at Delphi who delivered the oracle's pronouncement.

32. The brother is Chaerecrates (Xenophon, *Memorabilia* II.3.1).

the god be saying? What does his riddle mean?[33] For I'm only too aware that I've no claim to being wise in anything either great or small. What can he mean, then, by saying that I'm wisest? Surely he can't be lying: that isn't lawful[34] for him."

For a long time I was perplexed about what he meant. Then, very reluctantly, I proceeded to examine it in the following sort of way. I approached one of the people thought to be wise, assuming that in his company, if anywhere, I could refute the pronouncement and say to the oracle, "Here's someone wiser than I, yet you said I was wisest."

Then I examined this person—there's no need for me to mention him by name; he was one of our politicians. And when I examined him and talked with him, men of Athens, my experience was something like this: I thought this man seemed wise to many people, and especially to himself, but wasn't. Then I tried to show him that he thought himself wise, but wasn't. As a result, he came to dislike me, and so did many of the people present. For my part, I thought to myself as I left, "I'm wiser than that person. For it's likely that neither of us knows anything fine and good, but he thinks he knows something he doesn't know, whereas I, since I don't in fact know, don't think that I do either. At any rate, it seems that I'm wiser than he in just this one small way: that what I don't know, I don't think I know." Next, I approached another man, one of those thought to be wiser than the first, and it seemed to me that the same thing occurred, and so I came to be disliked by that man too, as well as by many others.

After that, then, I kept approaching one person after another. I realized, with distress and alarm, that I was arousing hostility. Nevertheless, I thought I must attach the greatest importance to what pertained to the god. So, in seeking what the oracle meant, I had to go to all those with any reputation for knowledge. And, by the dog,[35] men of Athens—for I'm obliged to tell the truth before you—I really did experience something like this: in my investigation in response to

33. Many of the attested Delphic pronouncements were riddles. Delphi seems to have encouraged care in their interpretation, treating a cavalier acceptance of them at face value as an example of the hubris it condemned.

34. What is lawful (*themis*) in the relevant sense accords with the divine law embodied in the universe, in contravention of which nothing can occur. See 30c8–d1.

35. Probably the dog-headed Egyptian god Anubis (see *Gorgias* 482b5; Aristophanes, *Wasps* 83). The oath is an emphatic one, like "my goodness" or "by all that's holy," with no particular religious significance.

the god, I found that, where wisdom is concerned, those who had
the best reputations were practically the most deficient, whereas men
5   who were thought to be their inferiors were much better off.[36]
Accordingly, I must present all my wanderings to you as if they were
labors[37] of some sort that I undertook in order to prove the oracle
utterly irrefutable.

You see, after the politicians, I approached the poets—tragic,
22b dithyrambic,[38] and the rest—thinking that in their company I'd catch
myself in the very act of being more ignorant than they. So I examined the poems with which they seemed to me to have taken the
most trouble and questioned them about what they meant, in order
that I might also learn something from them at the same time.[39]

5   Well, I'm embarrassed to tell you the truth, gentlemen, but nevertheless it must be told. In a word, almost all the people present could
have discussed these poems better than their authors themselves. And
so, in the case of the poets as well, I soon realized it wasn't wisdom
that enabled them to compose their poems, but some sort of natural
22c inspiration, of just the sort you find in prophets and soothsayers.[40] For
these people, too, say many fine things, but know nothing of what
they speak about. The poets also seemed to me to be in this sort of
situation. At the same time, I realized that, because of their poetry,
5   they thought themselves to be the wisest of people about the other
things as well[41] when they weren't. So I left their company, too,

---

36. That is, the craftsmen were better off regarding wisdom than the poets or politicians (see 22c9–d3).

37. Presumably a reference to the so-called labors of Heracles. See *Euthyphro* 4a11
note.

38. A dithyramb was a choral song in honor of the god Dionysus.

39. That is, at the same time as investigating the meaning of the oracle.

40. See *Meno* 99b5–c5: "It's not by any sort of wisdom, then, that [men famous for
their political ability] . . . guided their cities; and that is also why they aren't able to
make others like themselves, because it's not on account of knowledge that they
are like that. . . . Then, if it's not by knowledge, true opinion becomes the remaining alternative; it's by using *this* that politicians guide their cities correctly, though
they are no different as regards wisdom than soothsayers and seers. For they too say
many true things while inspired, but they know nothing about any of the things
they say." Poetic inspiration is further discussed in the *Ion* (see especially 534c5–6).

41. Namely, "the most important things" (22d6–8), identified as wisdom, truth,
and the best possible state of the soul (29e1–30a2) and as "just and fine and good
and advantageous things" (*Alcibiades* I 118a7–12).

thinking that I had gotten the better of them in the very same way as of the politicians.

Finally, I approached the craftsmen. You see, I was conscious of knowing practically nothing myself, but I knew I'd discover that they, at least, would know many fine things. And I wasn't wrong about this. On the contrary, they did know things that I didn't know, and in that respect they were wiser than I. But, men of Athens, the good crafts- men also seemed to me to have the very same flaw as the poets: because he performed his own craft well, each of them also thought himself to be wisest about the other things, the most important ones; and this error of theirs seemed to overshadow their wisdom. So I asked myself on behalf of the oracle whether I'd prefer to be as I am, not in any way wise with their wisdom nor ignorant with their ignorance, or to have both qualities as they did. And the answer I gave to myself, and to the oracle, was that it profited me more to be just the way I was.

From this examination, men of Athens, much hostility has arisen against me of a sort that is harshest and most onerous. This has resulted in many slanders, including that reputation I mentioned of being "wise." You see, the people present on each occasion think that I'm wise about the subjects on which I examine others. But in fact, gentlemen, it's pretty certainly the god who is really wise, and by his oracle he meant that human wisdom[42] is worth little or nothing. And it seems that when he refers to the Socrates here before you and uses my name, he makes me an example, as if he were to say, "That one among you is wisest, mortals, who, like Socrates, has recognized that he's truly worthless where wisdom's concerned."

So even now I continue to search and to examine, in response to the god, any person, citizen, or foreigner I believe to be wise. When- ever he seems not to be so to me, I come to the assistance of the god and show him that he's not wise. Because of this occupation, I've had no leisure worth talking about for either the city's affairs or my own domestic ones; rather, I live in extreme poverty because of my service to the god.

In addition to these factors, the young people who follow me around of their own accord,[43] those who have the most leisure, the sons of the very rich, enjoy listening to people being cross-examined.

22d

5

22e

5

23a

5

23b

5

23c

---

42. See 20d7–8.

43. Reading μοι ⟨οἱ⟩ ἐπακολουθοῦντες with de Strycker and Slings.

They often imitate me themselves and in turn attempt to cross-exam-
5   ine others. Next, I imagine they find an abundance of people who
think they possess some knowledge, but in fact know little or nothing. The result is that those they question are angry not at themselves,
23d   but at me, and say that Socrates is a thoroughly pestilential[44] fellow
who corrupts the young. Then, when they're asked what he's doing
or teaching, they've nothing to say, as they don't know. Yet, so as not
to appear at a loss, they utter the stock phrases used against all who
5   philosophize: "things in the sky and beneath the earth," and "not
acknowledging the gods," and "making the weaker argument the
stronger." For they wouldn't be willing to tell the truth, I imagine:
that it has become manifest they pretend to know, but know nothing.
So, seeing that these people are, I imagine, ambitious, vehement, and
23e   numerous, and have been speaking earnestly and persuasively about
me, they've long been filling your ears with vehement slanders. On
the basis of these slanders, Meletus has brought his charges against
me, and Anytus and Lycon[45] along with him: Meletus is aggrieved on
5   behalf of the poets, Anytus on behalf of the artisans and politicians,
24a   and Lycon on behalf of the orators. So, as I began by saying, I'd be
amazed if I could rid your minds of this slander in the brief time
available, when there's so much of it in them.

There, men of Athens, is the truth for you. I've spoken it without
concealing or glossing over anything, whether great or small. And yet
I pretty much know that I make enemies by doing these very
things.[46] And that's further evidence that I'm right—that this is the
prejudice against me and these its causes. Whether you investigate
24b   these matters now or later, you'll find it to be so.

Enough, then, for my defense before you against the charges brought
by my first accusers. Next, I'll try to defend myself against Meletus—
who is, he claims, both good and patriotic—and against my later
5   accusers. Once again, then, just as if they were really a different set of
accusers, their affidavit must be examined in turn. It goes something
like this:

---

44. *Miarōtatos*: carries the connotation of being polluted or contaminated (in Socrates' case, by the impiety of atheism) and of being a threat to others as a result.
See *Euthyphro* 4c1–3 and note.

45. Otherwise unknown.

46. Reading αὐτοῖς τούτοις with Burnet.

Socrates is guilty of corrupting the young, and of not acknowledging the gods the city acknowledges, but new daimonic activities
instead.[47]

Such, then, is the charge. Let us examine each point in this charge.   24c
Meletus says, then, that I commit injustice by corrupting the
young. But I, men of Athens, reply that it's Meletus who is guilty of   5
playing around with serious matters, of lightly bringing people to
trial, and of professing to be seriously concerned about things he has
never cared about at all—and I'll try to prove this.[48]

Step forward, Meletus, and answer me. You regard it as most
important, do you not, that our young people be as good as possible?
I certainly do.   24d
Come, then, and tell these jurors who improves them. Clearly you
know, since you care. For having discovered, as you assert, the one

---

47. *Daimonia*: the neuter plural of the adjective *daimonios*. The exchange at 27b4–
28a2 shows that it refers here to the activities—specifically, to the spoken prohi-
bitions (31c7–d4)—of substantive daimons, who are themselves either gods or the
offspring of gods and mortals.

48. Under Athenian law, any citizen could bring an indictment against another
whom he believed to be guilty of wrongdoing. As a result, a citizen who brought
such a legal action typically played two roles, which in our system of criminal law
are kept separate, that of prosecutor and that of chief witness for the prosecution.
Meletus is both charging Socrates with impiety, therefore, and attesting (together
with Anytus and Lycon) that he did specific impious things. This is made clear by
the fact that he called no other witnesses beyond his fellow accusers to support his
case (34a2–6, 36a7–b2). Meletus' indictment is both a charge, then, and a sworn
affidavit supporting the charge. It follows that Meletus must be the final authority
on what that charge amounts to, just as a witness is the final authority on what his
testimony means. It's clear, therefore, that Socrates' primary responsibility must be
to answer the charges *as they are interpreted by Meletus* and not, as would be the case
in our legal system, the written charges identified in some other way (e.g., by stat-
ute). Moreover, because Meletus is as much a witness as a prosecutor, because his
indictment is both affidavit and charge, Athenian law allows Socrates to cross-examine him and obliges Meletus to answer his questions (27b3–c7). Hence Socrates
can attack Meletus' indictment by discrediting him as a witness, by showing that
he does not know enough about the things in his indictment for his testimony to
carry any weight (think of how witnesses are discredited in our own legal system).
This explains—what would otherwise be a complete mystery—why the professed
aim of Socrates' examination of Meletus is as he describes it here. For if Socrates
can achieve his aim, he will have seriously undermined not just Meletus, but his
testimony and charges too.

who corrupts them—namely, myself—you bring him before these
5 jurors and accuse him. Come, then, speak up, tell the jurors who it is
that improves them. Do you see, Meletus, that you remain silent and
have nothing to say? Yet don't you think that's shameful and sufficient
evidence of exactly what I say, that you care nothing at all? Speak up,
my good man. Who improves them?

10 The laws.

But that's not what I'm asking, my most excellent fellow, but
24e rather which *person*, who knows the laws themselves in the first place,
does this?

These gentlemen, Socrates, the jurors.

What are you saying, Meletus? Are they able to educate and
5 improve the young?

Most certainly.

All of them, or some but not others?

All of them.

That's good news, by Hera,[49] and a great abundance of benefactors
that you speak of! What, then, about the audience present here? Do
25a they improve the young or not?

Yes, they do so too.

And what about the members of the Council?[50]

Yes, the councilors too.

But, if that's so, Meletus, surely those in the Assembly, the assem-
5 blymen, won't corrupt the young, will they? Won't they all improve
them too?

Yes, they will too.

But then it seems that all the Athenians except for me make young
people fine and good, whereas I alone corrupt them. Is that what
10 you're saying?

Most emphatically, that's what I'm saying.

I find myself, if you're right, in a most unfortunate situation. Now
answer me this. Do you think that the same holds of horses? Do people
25b in general improve them, whereas one particular person corrupts them

---

49. See *Euthyphro* 8b4 note.

50. The Council consisted of 500 male citizens over the age of 30, elected annually by lot, 50 from each of the 10 tribes of Athens (32b2 note). The Council met
daily (except for some holidays and the like) as a steering committee for the Assembly (*Euthyphro* 3c1 note). Its responsibilities included state finance, public
buildings, and the equipment of navy and cavalry.

or makes them worse? Or isn't it wholly the opposite: one particular person—or the very few who are horse trainers—is able to improve them, whereas the majority of people, if they have to do with horses and make use of them, make them worse? Isn't that true, Meletus, both of horses and of all other animals? Of course it is, whether you and Anytus   5
say so or not. Indeed, our young people are surely in a very happy situation if only one person corrupts them, whereas all the rest benefit them.

Well then, Meletus, it has been adequately established that you've   25c
never given any thought to young people—you've plainly revealed your indifference—and that you care nothing about the issues on which you bring me to trial.

Next, Meletus, tell us, in the name of Zeus, whether it's better to live among good citizens or bad ones. Answer me, sir. Surely, I'm not asking you anything difficult. Don't bad people do something bad to whoever's closest to them at the given moment, whereas good people do something good?

Certainly.   10

Now is there anyone who wishes to be harmed rather than bene-   25d
fited by those around him? Keep answering, my good fellow. For the law requires you to answer. Is there anyone who wishes to be harmed?

Of course not.   5

Well, then, when you summon me here for corrupting the young and making them worse, do you mean that I do so intentionally or unintentionally?

Intentionally, *I* say.

What's that, Meletus? Are you so much wiser at your age than I at mine, that you know bad people do something bad to whomever's   10
closest to them at the given moment, and good people something good? Am I, by contrast, so very ignorant that I don't know even this: 25e
that if I do something bad to an associate, I risk getting back something bad from him in return? And is the result, as you claim, that I do so very bad a thing intentionally?

I'm not convinced by you of that, Meletus, and neither, I think, is anyone else. No, either I'm not corrupting the young or, if I am corrupting them, it's *un*intentionally, so that in either case what you say is   26a
false. But if I'm corrupting them unintentionally, the law doesn't require that I be brought to court for such mistakes—that is, unintentional ones[51]—but that I be taken aside for private instruction and

---

51. Reading καὶ ἀκουσίων with the mss.

admonishment. For it's clear that if I'm instructed, I'll stop doing what I do unintentionally. You, however, avoided associating with me and were unwilling to instruct me. Instead, you bring me here, where the law requires you to bring those in need of punishment, not instruction.

Well, men of Athens, what I said before is absolutely clear by this point, namely, that Meletus has never cared about these matters to any extent, great or small. Nevertheless, please tell us now, Meletus, how is it you say I corrupt the young? Or is it absolutely clear, from the indictment you wrote, that it's by teaching them not to acknowledge the gods the city acknowledges, but new daimonic activities instead? Isn't that what you say I corrupt them by teaching?

I most emphatically do say that.

Then, in the name of those very gods we're now discussing, Meletus, speak yet more clearly, both for my sake and for that of these gentlemen. You see, I'm unable to tell what you mean. Is it that I teach people to acknowledge that some gods exist—so that I, then, acknowledge their existence myself and am not an out-and-out atheist and am not guilty of that—yet not, of course, the very ones acknowledged by the city, but different ones? Is that what you're charging me with, that they're different ones? Or are you saying that I myself don't acknowledge any gods at all, and that that's what I teach to others?

That's what I mean, that you don't acknowledge any gods at all.

You're a strange fellow, Meletus! What makes you say that? Do I not even acknowledge that the sun and the moon are gods, then, as other men do?

No, by Zeus, gentlemen of the jury, he doesn't, since he says that the sun's a stone and the moon earth.

My dear Meletus, do you think it's Anaxagoras[52] you're accusing? Are you that contemptuous of the jury? Do you think they're so illiterate that they don't know that the books of Anaxagoras of Clazomenae are full of such arguments? And, in particular, do young people

52. Anaxagoras of Clazomenae (c. 500–428 B.C.E.) settled in Athens (c. 456 B.C.E.) where he remained until he fled to Lampsacus to escape indictment for impiety (c. 436 B.C.E.). He was a friend of the great Athenian statesman Pericles, and the indictment may have been motivated at least in part by political hostility to the latter. Anaxagoras accorded a fundamental cosmological role to (divine) Mind. His views are criticized at *Phaedo* 97b8–99d2.

learn these views from me, views they can occasionally acquire in the   10
Orchestra[53] for a drachma at most and that they'd ridicule Socrates for   26e
pretending were his own—especially as they're so strange? In the
name of Zeus, is that really how I seem to you? Do I acknowledge
the existence of no god at all?

No indeed, by Zeus, none at all.   5

You aren't at all convincing, Meletus, not even, it seems to me, to
yourself. You see, men of Athens, this fellow seems very arrogant and
intemperate to me and to have written this indictment simply out of
some sort of arrogance, intemperance, and youthful rashness.[54]
Indeed, he seems to have composed a sort of riddle in order to test
me: "Will the so-called wise Socrates recognize that I'm playing   27a
around and contradicting myself? Or will I fool him along with the
other listeners?" You see, he seems to me to be contradicting himself   5
in his indictment, as if he were to say, "Socrates is guilty of not
acknowledging gods, but of acknowledging gods." And that's just
childish playing around, isn't it?

Please examine with me, gentlemen, why it seems to me that this
is what he's saying. And you, Meletus, answer us. But you, gentlemen, please remember what I asked of you at the beginning: don't   10
create an uproar if I make my arguments in my accustomed manner.   27b

Is there anyone, Meletus, who acknowledges that human activities
exist but doesn't acknowledge human beings? Make him answer, gentlemen, and don't let him make one protest after another. Is there   5
anyone who doesn't acknowledge horses but does acknowledge
equine activities? Or who doesn't acknowledge that musicians[55] exist
but does acknowledge musical activities? There's no one, best of
men—if you don't want to answer, I must answer for you and for the
others here. But at least answer my next question. Is there anyone
who acknowledges the existence of daimonic activities but doesn't   27c
acknowledge daimons?

No, there isn't.

How good of you to answer, if reluctantly and when compelled to
by these gentlemen. Well then, you say that I acknowledge daimonic

---

53. The Orchestra was part of the marketplace (*agora*) in Athens. What was available for a drachma was probably not Anaxagoras' book, but a recitation of its
contents.

54. See 17c5 and note.

55. Literally, aulos players. The aulos was a reed instrument rather like an oboe.

5 activities, whether new or familiar, and teach about them. But then,
on your account, I do at any rate acknowledge daimonic activities,
and to this you've sworn in your indictment against me. However, if I
acknowledge daimonic activities, surely it's absolutely necessary that I
acknowledge daimons. Isn't that so? Yes, it is—I assume you agree,
10 since you don't answer. But don't we believe that daimons are either
27d gods or, at any rate, children of gods? Yes or no?

Of course.

Then, if indeed I do believe in daimons, as you're saying, and if
daimons are gods of some sort, that's precisely what I meant when I
5 said that you're presenting us with a riddle and playing around: you're
saying that I don't believe in gods and, on the contrary, that I do
believe in gods, since in fact I do at least believe in daimons. But if,
on the other hand, daimons are children of gods, some sort of bastard
offspring of a nymph, or of whomever else tradition says each one is
the child, what man could possibly believe that children of gods exist,
10 but not gods? That would be just as unreasonable as believing in the
27e children of horses and asses[56]—namely, mules—while not believing
in the existence of horses and asses.

Well then, Meletus, you must have written these things to test us[57]
or because you were at a loss about what genuine injustice to charge
me with. There's no conceivable way you could persuade any man
with even the slightest intelligence that the same person believes in
both daimonic activities and gods, and, on the contrary, that this same
28a person believes neither in daimons, nor in gods, nor in heroes.[58]

In fact, then, men of Athens, it doesn't seem to me to require a
long defense to show that I'm not guilty of the charges in Meletus'
indictment, but what I've said is sufficient. But what I was also saying
5 earlier, that much hostility has arisen against me and among many
people—you may be sure that's true. And *it's* what will convict me, if
I am convicted: not Meletus or Anytus, but the slander and malice of
many people. It has certainly convicted many other good men as
28b well, and I imagine it will do so again. There's no danger it will stop
with me.

---

56. Omitting ἤ with de Strycker and Slings.

57. Omitting τὴν γραφὴν ταύτην with de Strycker and Slings.

58. Heroes are demigods (28c2), children of gods and mortals, whose existence
therefore entails the existence of gods. Hence someone who denies the existence
of gods denies that of heroes too.

But perhaps someone may say, "Aren't you ashamed, Socrates, to have engaged in the sort of occupation that has now put you at risk of death?" I, however, would be right to reply to him, "You're not think- 5 ing straight, sir, if you think that a man who's any use at all should give any opposing weight to the risk of living or dying, instead of looking to this alone whenever he does anything: whether his actions are just or unjust, the deeds of a good or bad man. You see, on your account, 28c all those demigods who died on the plain of Troy were inferior people, especially the son of Thetis, who was so contemptuous of danger when the alternative was something shameful.⁵⁹ When he was eager to kill Hector, his mother, since she was a goddess, spoke to him, I think, in 5 some such words as these: 'My child, if you avenge the death of your friend Patroclus and slay Hector, you will die yourself immediately,' so the poem goes, 'as your death is fated to follow next after Hector's.' But though he heard that, he was contemptuous of death and danger, for he was far more afraid of living as a bad man and of failing to 10 avenge his friends: 'Let me die immediately, then,' it continues, 'once 28d I've given the wrongdoer his just deserts,⁶⁰ so that I do not remain here by the curved ships, a laughingstock and a burden upon the earth.' Do you really suppose he gave a thought to death or danger?"

You see, men of Athens, this is the truth of the matter: Wherever someone has stationed himself because he thinks it best, or wherever 5 he's been stationed by his commander, there, it seems to me, he should remain, steadfast in danger, taking no account at all of death or of anything else, in comparison to what's shameful. I'd therefore have been acting scandalously, men of Athens, if, when I'd been stationed 28e in Potidea, Amphipolis, or Delium⁶¹ by the leaders you had elected to lead me, I had, like many another, remained where they'd stationed me and run the risk of death. But if, when the god stationed me here, as I became thoroughly convinced he did, to live practicing philoso- phy, examining myself and others, I had—for fear of death or any- thing else—abandoned my station. 29a

---

59. See Homer, *Iliad* XVIII.94 ff. Thetis' son, born of a mortal father, Peleus, and hence a demigod, is Achilles.

60. "Once I've given . . . deserts" is a Socratic addition to Homer's text.

61. Three battles in the Peloponnesian War between Athens and its allies and Sparta and its allies. See Thucydides I.56–65 (Potidaea), IV.90 (Delium), V.2 (Amphipolis). Socrates' bravery at Potidea and Delium is described at *Symposium* 219e5–221d6.

That would have been scandalous, and someone might have rightly and justly brought me to court for not acknowledging that gods exist, by disobeying the oracle, fearing death, and thinking I
5   was wise when I wasn't. You see, fearing death, gentlemen, is nothing other than thinking one is wise when one isn't, since it's thinking one knows what one doesn't know. I mean, no one knows whether death may not be the greatest of all goods for people, but they fear it as if they knew for certain that it's the worst thing of all. Yet surely[62]
29b   this is the most blameworthy ignorance of thinking one knows what one doesn't know. But I, gentlemen, may perhaps differ from most people by just this much in this matter too. And if I really were to claim to be wiser than anyone in any way, it would be in this: that as
5   I don't have adequate knowledge about things in Hades, so too I don't think that I have knowledge. To act unjustly, on the other hand, to disobey someone better than oneself, whether god or man, that I do know to be bad and shameful. In any case, I'll never fear or avoid things that may for all I know be good more than things I know are bad.

Suppose, then, you're prepared to let me go now and to disobey
29c   Anytus, who said I shouldn't have been brought to court at all,[63] but that since I had been brought to court, you had no alternative but to put me to death because, as he stated before you, if I were acquitted,
5   soon your sons would all be entirely corrupted by following Socrates' teachings. Suppose, confronted with that claim, you were to say to me, "Socrates, we will not obey Anytus this time. Instead, we are prepared to let you go. But on the following condition: that you spend no more time on this investigation and don't practice philosophy, and if you're caught doing so, you'll die." Well, as I just said, if you were to
29d   let me go on these terms, I'd reply to you, "I've the utmost respect and affection for you, men of Athens, but I'll obey the god rather than you, and as long as I draw breath and am able, I won't give up practicing philosophy, exhorting you and also showing the way[64] to any of you I ever happen to meet, saying just the sorts of things I'm accustomed to say:

---

62. Reading καίτοι with Eusebius.

63. Anytus presumably thought that Socrates would exile himself to escape trial, as Anaxagoras (26d6 note) had done. See *Crito* 45e3–4.

64. By showing you that you aren't wise though you think you are (23b7).

My excellent man, you're an Athenian, you belong to the greatest city, renowned for its wisdom and strength; are you not ashamed that you take care to acquire as much wealth as possible—and reputation and honor—but that about wisdom and truth, about how your soul may be in the best possible condition, you take neither care nor thought?

29e

Then, if one of you disagrees and says that he *does* care, I won't let him go away immediately, but I'll question, examine, and test him. And if he doesn't seem to me to possess virtue, though he claims he does, I'll reproach him, saying that he treats the most important things as having the least value, and inferior ones as having more. This I will do for anyone I meet, young or old, alien or fellow citizen— but especially for you, my fellow citizens, since you're closer kin to me. This, you may be sure, is what the god orders me to do. And I believe that no greater good for you has ever come about in the city than my service to the god. You see, I do nothing else except go around trying to persuade you, both young and old alike, not to care about your bodies or your money as intensely as about how your soul may be in the best possible condition. I say,

5

30a

5

30b

It's not from wealth that virtue comes, but from virtue comes money, and all the other things that are good for human beings, both in private and in public life.[65]

Now if by saying this, I'm corrupting the young, *this* is what you'd have to think to be harmful. But if anyone claims I say something other than this, he's talking nonsense."

5

"It's in that light," I want to say, "men of Athens, that you should obey Anytus or not, and let me go or not—knowing that I wouldn't act in any other way, not even if I were to die many times over."

30c

Don't create an uproar, men of Athens. Instead, please abide by my request not to create an uproar at what I say, but to listen. For I think it will profit you to listen. You see, I'm certainly going to say some

5

---

65. Since Socrates is a poor man (23b9, 31c2–3, 38b1–6), he is hardly saying that virtue inevitably brings a lot of money. Rather he is saying that virtue brings as much money as is a good thing, and this may not be very much. Only someone who believed that money was itself the best thing or that virtue was strictly moral virtue (18a5 note) could find this disquieting.

further things to you at which you may perhaps exclaim—but by no means do so.

You may be sure that if you put me to death—a man of the sort I said I was just now—you won't harm me more than you harm yourselves. Certainly, Meletus or Anytus couldn't harm me in any way: that's not possible. For I don't think it's lawful for a better man to be harmed by a worse.[66] He may, of course, kill me, or perhaps banish or disenfranchise me. And these *he* believes to be very bad things, and others no doubt agree. But *I* don't believe this. Rather, I believe that doing what he's doing now—attempting to kill a man unjustly—is far worse.

So, men of Athens, I'm far from pleading in my own defense now, as might be supposed. Instead, I'm pleading in yours, so that you don't commit a great wrong against the god's gift to you by condemning me. If you put me to death, you won't easily find another like me. For, even if it seems ridiculous to say so, I've literally been attached to the city, as if to a large thoroughbred horse that was somewhat sluggish because of its size and needed to be awakened by some sort of gadfly. It's as just such a gadfly, it seems to me, that the god has attached me to the city—one that awakens, persuades, and reproaches each and every one of you and never stops alighting everywhere on you the whole day. You won't easily find another like that, gentlemen. So if you obey me, you'll spare my life. But perhaps you'll be resentful, like people awakened from a doze, and slap at me. If you obey Anytus, you might easily kill me. Then you might spend the rest of your lives asleep, unless the god, in his compassion for you, were to send you someone else.

That I am indeed the sort of person to be given as a gift to the city by the god, you may recognize from this: it doesn't seem a merely human matter—does it?—for me to have neglected all my own affairs and to have put up with this neglect of my domestic life for so many years now, but always to have minded your business, by visiting each of you in private, like a father or elder brother, to persuade you to care about virtue. Of course, if I were getting anything out of it or if I were being paid for giving this advice, my conduct would be intelligible. But, as it is, you can plainly see for yourselves that my accusers, who so shamelessly accused me of everything else, couldn't bring themselves to be so utterly shameless as to call a witness to say that I ever once

---

66. For the meaning of "lawful" (*themiton*), see 21b6 note. The confident—and puzzling—claim is partly explained at *Crito* 44d8–10 and note.

accepted or asked for payment. In fact, it's *I* who can call what I think   31c
is a sufficient witness that I'm telling the truth—my poverty.

But perhaps it may seem strange that I, of all people, give this advice
by going around and minding other people's business in private, yet   5
do not venture to go before your Assembly and give advice to the city
in public. The reason for that, however, is one you've heard me give
many times and in many places: A divine and daimonic thing comes
to me—the very thing Meletus made mocking allusion to in the
indictment he wrote. It's something that began happening to me in   31d
childhood: a sort of voice comes, which, whenever it does come,
always holds me back from what I'm about to do but never urges me
forward. *It* is what opposes my engaging in politics—and to me, at   5
least, its opposition seems entirely right. For you may be sure, men of
Athens, that if I'd[67] tried to engage in politics I'd have perished long
ago and have benefited neither you nor myself.

Please don't resent me if I tell you the truth. The fact is that no   31e
man will be spared by you or by any other multitude of people if he
genuinely opposes a lot of unjust and unlawful actions and tries to
prevent them from happening in the city. On the contrary, anyone
who really fights for what's just, if indeed he's going to survive for   32a
even a short time, must act privately not publicly.

I'll present substantial evidence of that—not words, but what you
value, deeds. Listen, then, to what happened to me, so you may see   5
that fear of death wouldn't lead me to submit to a single person contrary to what's just, not even if I were to perish at once for not submitting. The things I'll tell you are of a vulgar sort commonly heard
in the law courts, but they're true nonetheless.

You see, men of Athens, I never held any other public office in the
city, but I've served on the Council. And it happened that my own   32b
tribe, Antiochis, was presiding[68] when you wanted[69] to try the ten
generals—the ones who failed to rescue the survivors of the naval

---

67. Omitting πάλαι with Cobet.

68. A *phulē* is not a tribe in our sense, but an administrative division of the citizen
body, most probably of military origin. The presiding committee of the Council
(25a3 note) consisted of the fifty members of one of the ten tribes, selected by lot
to serve for one-tenth of the year. It arranged meetings of the Council and Assembly, received envoys and letters to the state, and conducted other routine business.

69. Reading ἐβούλεσθε with de Strycker and Slings.

battle—as a group.[70] That was unlawful, as you all came to recognize
5   at a later time. On that occasion, I was the only presiding member
opposed to your doing something illegal, and I voted against you.
And though the orators[71] were ready to lay information against me
and have me summarily arrested,[72] and you were shouting and urging
them on, I thought that I should face danger on the side of law and
32c   justice, rather than go along with you for fear of imprisonment or
death when your proposals were unjust.

ThisI happened when the city was still under democratic rule. But
later, when the oligarchy had come to power, it happened once more.
The Thirty[73] summoned me and four others to the Tholus[74] and
5   ordered us to arrest Leon of Salamis[75] and bring him from Salamis to
die. They gave many such orders to many other people too, of course,
since they wanted to implicate as many as possible in their crimes. On
that occasion, however, I showed once again not by words but by
32d   deeds that I couldn't care less about death—if that isn't putting it too
bluntly—but that all I care about is not doing anything unjust or
impious. You see, that government, powerful though it was, didn't
5   frighten me into unjust action: when we came out of the Tholus, the
other four went to Salamis and arrested Leon, whereas I left and went
home. I might have died for that if the government hadn't fallen
shortly afterward.

---

70. After the naval battle at Arginusae on the Ionian coast of Asia Minor (406
B.C.E.), ten Athenian generals were indicted for failing to rescue survivors and pick
up the bodies of the dead. Both Council and Assembly voted to try them as a
group, which was against Athenian law. See Xenophon, *Hellenica* I.7.

71. The politicians supporting the mass trial.

72. *Endeiknunai . . . kai apagein*: *Endeixis* (lay information against) and *apagoge* (have
summarily arrested) were formal legal actions of a specific sort.

73. After Athens was defeated by Sparta in 404 B.C.E., its democratic government
was replaced by a brutal oligarchy, the so-called Thirty Tyrants, which survived
barely eight months. During that time it allegedly executed some fifteen hundred
people, and many more went into exile to escape. Two members of the Thirty—
Critias and Charmides—were relatives of Plato's and appear as Socratic interlocutors in the dialogues named after them. Socrates' association with them is often
thought to have been one of the things that led to his indictment.

74. The Tholus was a dome-shaped building, also called the Skias ("parasol"). The
presiding committee of the Council (32b2 note) took its meals there.

75. Leon is otherwise unknown. The episode, however, is widely reported (*Seventh Letter* 324d8–325c5; Xenophon, *Hellenica* II.3.39, *Memorabilia* IV.4.3).

There are many witnesses who will testify before you about these
events.   32e

Do you imagine, then, that I'd have survived all these years if I'd
been regularly active in public affairs, and had come to the aid of justice like a good man, and regarded that as most important, as one
should? Far from it, men of Athens, and neither would any other   5
man. But throughout my entire life, in any public activities I may   33a
have engaged in, it was evident I was the sort of person—and in private life I was the same—who never agreed to anything with anyone
contrary to justice, whether with others or with those who my slanderers[76] say are my students. In fact, I've never been anyone's teacher   5
at any time. But if anyone, whether young or old, wanted to listen to
me while I was talking and performing my own task, I never
begrudged that to him. Neither do I engage in conversation only
when I receive a fee and not when I don't. Rather, I offer myself for   33b
questioning to rich and poor alike, or, if someone prefers, he may listen to me and answer my questions. And if any one of these turned
out well, or did not do so, I can't justly be held responsible, since I
never at any time promised any of them that they'd learn anything   5
from me or that I'd teach them. And if anyone says that he learned
something from me or heard something in private that all the others
didn't also hear, you may be sure he isn't telling the truth.[77]

Why, then, you may ask, do some people enjoy spending so much
time with me? You've heard the answer, men of Athens. I told you the   33c
whole truth: it's because they enjoy listening to people being examined
who think they're wise but aren't. For it's not unpleasant. In my case,
however, it's something, you may take it from me, I've been ordered to
do by the god, in both oracles and dreams, and in every other way that   5
divine providence ever ordered any man to do anything at all.

All these things, men of Athens, are both true and easily tested. I
mean, if I really do corrupt the young or have corrupted them in the
past, surely if any of them had recognized when they became older   33d
that I'd given them bad advice at some point in their youth, they'd
now have come forward themselves to accuse me and seek redress.
Or else, if they weren't willing to come themselves, some of their   5
family members—fathers, brothers, or other relatives—if indeed

---

76. Reading οὕς δὴ οἱ διαβάλλοντες ἐμέ with de Strycker and Slings.
77. See Aristophanes, *Clouds* 140–144.

their kinsmen had suffered any harm from me—would remember it
now and seek redress.

    In any case, I see many of these people present here: first of all,
10 there's Crito, my contemporary and fellow demesman, the father of
33e   Critobulus here;[78] then there's Lysanius of Sphettus, father of
Aeschines here;[79] next, there's Epigenes' father, Antiphon of Cephisia
here.[80] Then there are others whose brothers have spent time in this
way: Nicostratus, son of Theozotides,[81] brother of Theodotus—by the
5   way, Theodotus is dead, so that Nicostratus is at any rate not being
held back by him;[82] and Paralius here, son of Demodocus, whose
brother was Theages;[83] and there's Adeimantus, the son of Ariston,
34a   whose brother is Plato here,[84] and Aeantodorus, whose brother here
is Apollodorus.[85] And there are many others I could mention, some of

---

78. Crito was a well-off farm owner (*Euthydemus* 291e8), able and willing to help
his friends financially (38b7, *Crito* 44b6–c5; Diogenes Laertius II.20–21, 31, 105,
121). His relationship with Socrates is that of an old close friend and neighbor,
who is also to some degree a patron or benefactor (Diogenes Laertius II.121) and
adviser on practical matters. Of Socrates' various friends, he is the one who takes
the lead, acting naturally as the spokesman of the others (*Crito* 43c5–8; *Phaedo*
115b5–118a14 below). Both belonged to the deme (see *Euthyphro* 2b9 note)
Alopeke. Critobulus, his son, was also a member of Socrates' circle and was
present at his death (*Phaedo* 59b7).

79. Aeschines of Sphettus (fourth-century B.C.E.) was a devoted follower of Socrates, present at his death (*Phaedo* 59b8). He taught oratory and wrote both
speeches for the law courts and Socratic dialogues, only fragments of which are
extant. His father is otherwise unknown.

80. Epigenes was present at Socrates' death (*Phaedo* 59b8) and was a member of
his circle (Xenophon, *Memorabilia* III.12). Neither he nor his father are otherwise
known.

81. Theozotides introduced two important democratic reforms after the fall of the
Thirty Tyrants (32c4 note). His sons are otherwise unknown.

82. Presumably from accusing Socrates on his behalf.

83. Otherwise largely unknown. Spurious works in the Platonic canon are named
after Theages and Demodocus.

84. This is one of three places in his dialogues that Plato mentions himself—38b6
and *Phaedo* 59b10 are the others. Adeimantus, with his brother Glaucon, plays an
important role in the *Republic*.

85. Apollodorus, an enthusiastic follower of Socrates, given to emotion (*Phaedo*
59a8–b1, 117c3–d6), is the narrator in the *Symposium*. His brother is otherwise
unknown.

whom Meletus most certainly ought to have called as witnesses in the course of his own speech. If he forgot to do so, let him call them now—I yield time to him. Let him tell us if he has any such witness. No, it's entirely the opposite, gentlemen. You'll find that they're all prepared to come to my aid, their corruptor, the one who, Meletus and Anytus claim, is doing harm to their families. Of course, the corrupted ones themselves might indeed have reason to come to my aid. But the *un*corrupted ones, their relatives, who are older men now, what reason could they possibly have to support me, other than the right and just one: that they know perfectly well that Meletus is lying, whereas I am telling the truth?

Well then, gentlemen, those, and perhaps other similar things, are pretty much all I have to say in my defense. But perhaps one of you might be resentful when he recalls his own behavior. Perhaps when he was contesting even a lesser charge than this charge, he positively entreated the jurors with copious tears, bringing forward his children and many other relatives and friends as well, in order to arouse as much pity as possible. And then he finds that I'll do none of these things, not even when I'm facing what might be considered the ultimate danger. Perhaps someone with these thoughts might feel more willful where I'm concerned and, made angry by these very same thoughts, cast his vote in anger. Well, if there's someone like that among you—of course, I don't expect there to be, but *if* there is—I think it appropriate for me to answer him as follows: "I do indeed have relatives, my excellent man. As Homer puts it,[86] I too 'wasn't born from oak or from rock' but from human parents. And so I do have relatives, sons too, men of Athens, three of them, one already a young man while two are still children. Nonetheless, I won't bring any of them forward here and then entreat you to vote for my acquittal."

Why, you may ask, will I do none of these things? Not because I'm willful, men of Athens, or want to dishonor you—whether I'm boldly facing death or not is a separate story. The point has to do with reputation—yours and mine and that of the entire city: it doesn't seem noble to me to do these things, especially at my age and with my reputation—for whether truly or falsely, it's firmly believed in any case that Socrates is superior to the majority of people in some way.

---

86. *Odyssey* XIX.163. Penelope is speaking to her husband, Odysseus (41c1 note), whom she hasn't yet recognized.

Therefore, if those of *you* who are believed to be superior—in either wisdom or courage or any other virtue whatever—behave like that, it would be shameful.

I've often seen people of this sort when they're on trial: they're
5 thought to be someone, yet they do astonishing things—as if they imagined they'd suffer something terrible if they died and would be immortal if only you didn't kill them. People like that seem to me to bring such shame to the city that any foreigner might well suppose
35b that those among the Athenians who are superior in virtue—the ones they select from among themselves for political office and other positions of honor—are no better than women.[87] I say this, men of Athens, because none of us[88] who are in any way whatever thought
5 to be someone should behave like that, nor, if we attempt to do so, should you allow it. On the contrary, you should make it clear you're far more likely to convict someone who makes the city despicable by staging these pathetic scenes than someone who minds his behavior.

10 Reputation aside, gentlemen, it doesn't seem just to me to entreat
35c the jury—nor to be acquitted by entreating it—but rather to inform it and persuade it. After all, a juror doesn't sit in order to grant justice as a favor, but to decide where justice lies. And he has sworn on oath not that he'll favor whomever he pleases, but that he'll judge accord-
5 ing to law.[89] We shouldn't accustom you to breaking your oath, then, nor should you become accustomed to doing so—neither of us would be doing something holy if we did. Hence don't expect me, men of Athens, to act toward you in ways I consider to be neither
35d noble, nor just, nor pious—most especially, by Zeus, when I'm being prosecuted for *impiety* by Meletus here. You see, if I tried to persuade and to force you by entreaties, after you've sworn an oath, I clearly would be teaching you not to believe in the existence of
5 gods, and my defense would literally convict me of not acknowledging gods. But that's far from being the case: I do acknowledge them, men of Athens, as none of my accusers does. I turn it over to you

---

87. Casual sexism of this sort is common in Plato's dialogues, but may reflect cultural rather than personal attitudes.

88. Reading ἡμᾶς.

89. The gist of this oath, which may be pieced together from references such as this one, was as follows: "I will judge according to the laws and decrees of Athens, and I will decide matters about which there are no laws by the most just opinion."

and to the god to judge me in whatever way will be best for me and for yourselves.[90]

•   •   •

There are many reasons, men of Athens, why I'm not resentful at this 35e outcome—that you voted to convict me—and this outcome wasn't unexpected by me. I'm much more surprised at the number of votes 36a cast on each side: I didn't think that the decision would be by so few votes but by a great many. Yet now, it seems, that if a mere thirty votes 5 had been cast differently, I'd have been acquitted.[91] Or rather, it seems to me that where Meletus is concerned I've been acquitted even as things stand. And not merely acquitted. On the contrary, one thing at least is clear to everyone: if Anytus had not come forward with Lycon to accuse me, Meletus would have been fined a thousand drachmas, since he wouldn't have received a fifth of the votes.[92] 36b

But be that as it may, the man demands the death penalty for me. Well then, what counterpenalty should I now propose to you, men of Athens? Or is it clear that it's whatever I deserve? What then should it be? What do I deserve to suffer or pay just because I didn't mind my 5 own business throughout my life? Because I didn't care about the things most people care about—making money, managing an estate, or being a general, a popular leader, or holding some other political office, or joining the cabals and factions that come to exist in a city— but thought myself too honest, in truth, to engage in these things and 36c survive? Because I didn't engage in things, if engaging in them was going to benefit neither you nor myself, but instead went to each of you privately and tried to perform what I claim is the greatest bene- faction? That was what I did. I tried to persuade each of you to care 5

---

90. The jury returns a guilty verdict. Meletus proposes the death penalty. The law permits Socrates to propose an alternative, or counterpenalty, which he proceeds to do in the next part of his defense. Later members of the jury will choose which- ever of the penalty and the counterpenalty they deem the more appropriate pun- ishment.

91. A jury of 500 (or 501) was usual for an indictment of impiety. It follows that the vote was 280 to 220, since a tied vote resulted in acquittal.

92. Socrates is imagining that his accusers received around 90 votes each, or a third of the 280 guilty votes. This is less than the 100 votes that Meletus needed to re- ceive in order to avoid paying the fine to which Socrates refers, which was insti- tuted by law to deter frivolous suits.

first not about any of his possessions, but about himself and how he'll become best and wisest; and not primarily about the city's possessions, but about the city itself; and to care about all other things in the same way.

36d

What, then, do I deserve to suffer for being such a man? Something good, men of Athens, if I'm indeed to propose a penalty that I truly deserve. Yes, and the sort of good thing, too, that would be appropriate for me. What, then, is appropriate for a poor man who is a public benefactor and needs to have the leisure to exhort you? Nothing could be more appropriate,[93] men of Athens, than for such a man to be given free meals in the Prytaneum—much more so for him, at any rate, than for anyone of you who has won a victory at Olympia, whether with a single horse or with a pair or a team of four.[94] You see, he makes you think you're happy, whereas I make you actually happy.[95] Besides, he doesn't need to be sustained in that way, but I do need it. So if, as justice demands, I must propose a penalty I deserve, that's the penalty I propose: free meals in the Prytaneum.

5

10

36e

37a

Now perhaps when I say this, you may think I'm speaking in a quite willful manner—just as when I talked about appeals to pity and supplications. That's not so, men of Athens, rather it's something like this: I'm convinced that I never intentionally do injustice to any man—but I can't get you to share my conviction, because we've talked together a short time. I say this, because if you had a law, as other men in fact do, not to try a capital charge in a single day, but over several, I think you'd be convinced.[96] But as things stand, it isn't easy to clear myself of huge slanders in a short time.

5

10

37b

Since *I'm* convinced that I've done injustice to no one, however, I'm certainly not likely to do myself injustice, to announce that I deserve something bad and to propose a penalty of that sort for myself. Why should I do that? In order not to suffer what Meletus

5

---

93. Omitting οὕτως with Adam.

94. The Prytaneum, a building on the northeast slope of the Acropolis, was the symbolic center of Athens, where the communal hearth was housed. See *Euthyphro* 3a7 note. Guests of the city and victors in the Olympic and other games were given free meals there.

95. Because "living well [being happy], living a fine life, and living justly are the same" (*Crito* 48b8); "wisdom is clearly virtue, either the whole of it or part of it" (*Meno* 87d2–89a5); and being examined by Socrates leads to human wisdom.

96. Sparta had a law of this sort.

proposes as a penalty for me, when I say that I don't know whether it's a good or a bad thing?[97] As an alternative to that, am I then to choose one of the things I know very well to be bad and propose it? Imprisonment, for example? And why should I live in prison, enslaved to the regularly appointed officers, the Eleven?[98] All right, a 37c fine with imprisonment until I pay? But in my case the effect would be precisely the one I just now described, since I haven't the means to pay.

Well then, should I propose exile? Perhaps that's what *you*'d pro- pose for me. But I'd certainly have to have an excessive love of life, 5 men of Athens, to be so irrational as to do that. I see that you, my fel- low citizens, were unable to tolerate my discourses and discussions but came to find them so burdensome and odious that you're now 37d seeking to get rid of them. Is it likely, then, that I'll infer that others will find them easy to bear? Far from it, men of Athens. It would be a fine life for me, indeed, a man of my age, to go into exile and spend his life exchanging one city for another, because he's always being expelled. You see, I well know that wherever I go, the young will 5 come to hear me speaking, just as they do here. And if I drive them away, they will themselves persuade their elders to expel me; whereas if I don't drive them away, their fathers and relatives will expel me 37e because of these same young people.

Now perhaps someone may say, "But by keeping quiet and mind- ing your own business, Socrates, wouldn't it be possible for you to live in exile for us?" This is the very hardest point on which to con- vince some of you. You see, if I say that to do *that* would be to dis- 5 obey the god, and that this is why I can't mind my own business, you won't believe me, since you'll suppose I'm being ironical.[99] But again, if I say it's the greatest good for a man to discuss virtue every 38a day, and the other things you've heard me discussing and examining myself and others about, on the grounds that the unexamined life[100] 5 isn't worth living for a human being, you'll believe me even less when I say that. But in fact, things are just as I claim them to be, men

---

97. See 29a–b.

98. Officials appointed by lot to be in charge of prisons and executions.

99. Ancient irony (*eirōneia*) involved not simply meaning the contrary of what one said, but saying it with the intention to deceive.

100. That is, a life left unexamined, whether by the person whose life it is or by someone else engaging the person in elenctic cross-examination.

of Athens, though it isn't easy to convince you of them. At the same time, I'm not accustomed to thinking that I deserve anything bad. If

38b I had the means, I'd have proposed a fine of as much as I could afford to pay, since that would have done me no harm at all. But as things stand, I don't have them—unless you want me to propose as much as

5 I'm in fact able to pay. Perhaps I could pay you about a mina of silver. So I propose a fine of that amount.

One moment, men of Athens. Plato here, and Crito, Critobulus, and Apollodorus as well, are urging me to propose thirty minas and saying that they themselves will guarantee it.[101] I propose a fine of that amount, therefore, and these men will be sufficient guarantors to

10 you of the silver.[102]

• • •

38c For the sake of a little time, men of Athens, you're going to earn from those who wish to denigrate our city both the reputation and the blame for having killed Socrates—that wise man. For those who wish to reproach you will, of course, claim that I'm wise, even if I'm

5 not. In any case,[103] if you'd waited a short time, this would have happened of its own accord. You, of course, see my age, you see that I'm already far along in life and close to death. I'm saying this not to all

38d of you, but to those who voted for the death penalty. And to those same people I also say this: Perhaps you imagine, gentlemen, that I

---

101. Thirty minas (three thousand silver drachmas) was almost ten years' salary for someone engaged in public works.

102. The jury votes for the death penalty, and Socrates begins the final part of his speech. He addresses one set of remarks to those who found him guilty (38c7–d2) and another to those who voted for the death penalty (39c1–2). This suggests that these two groups were not identical. The fact that he describes those who voted to acquit him as deserving to be called jurors (40a2–3) suggests there was no overlap between this group and the group who voted for death. For Socrates would hardly be likely to refer to the latter in such flattering terms. It follows that fewer jurors voted for the death penalty than voted guilty. This contradicts the claim made by Diogenes Laertius (2.42), some five centuries later, that there were eighty more votes for the sentence of death than for the verdict of guilty. But it's surely what we would expect. For jurors who believed Socrates to be innocent would hardly vote to put him to death, and some of those who did find him guilty are likely to have recoiled at the death penalty.

103. Reading οὖν with βδ.

was convicted for lack of the sort of arguments I could have used to
convince you, if I'd thought I should do or say anything to escape the
penalty. Far from it. I *have* been convicted for a lack—not of argu-   5
ments, however, but of boldfaced shamelessness and for being
unwilling to say the sorts of things to you you'd have been most
pleased to hear, with me weeping and wailing, and doing and saying
many other things I claim are unworthy of me, but that are the very
sorts of things you're used to hearing from everyone else. No, I didn't   38e
think then that I should do anything servile because of the danger I
faced, and so I don't regret now that I defended myself as I did. I'd far
rather die after such a defense than live like that.

You see, whether in a trial or in a war, neither I nor anyone else   5
should contrive to escape death at all costs. In battle, too, it often   **39a**
becomes clear that one might escape death by throwing down one's
weapons and turning to supplicate one's pursuers. And in each sort of
danger there are many other ways one can contrive to escape death, if   5
one is shameless enough to do or say anything. The difficult thing,
gentlemen, isn't escaping death; escaping villainy is much more difficult, since it runs faster than death. And now I, slow and old as I am,   **39b**
have been overtaken by the slower runner while my accusers, clever
and sharp-witted as they are, have been overtaken by the faster one—
vice. And now I take my leave, convicted by you of a capital crime,
whereas they stand forever convicted by the truth of wickedness and   5
injustice. And just as I accept my penalty, so must they. Perhaps, things
had to turn out this way, and I suppose it's good they have.

Next, I want to make a prophecy to those who convicted me.   **39c**
Indeed, I'm now at the point at which men prophesy most—when
they're about to die. I say to you men who condemned me to death
that as soon as I'm dead vengeance will come upon you, and it will be
much harsher, by Zeus, than the vengeance you take in killing me.   5
You did this now in the belief that you'll escape giving an account of
your lives. But I say that quite the opposite will happen to you. There
will be more people to test you, whom I now restrain, though you   **39d**
didn't notice my doing so. And they'll be all the harsher on you, since
they're younger, and you'll resent it all the more. You see, if you imagine that by killing people you'll prevent anyone from reproaching you
for not living in the right way, you're not thinking straight. In fact, to   5
escape is neither possible nor noble. On the contrary, what's best and
easiest isn't to put down other people, but to prepare oneself to be the

best one can. With that prophecy to those of you who voted to con-
10   vict me, I take my leave.

However, I'd gladly discuss this result with those who voted for my
39e   acquittal while the officers of the court are busy and I'm not yet on
my way to the place where I must die. Please stay with me, gentlemen, just for that short time. After all, there's nothing to prevent us
5   from having a talk with one another while it's still in our power. To
40a   you whom I regard as friends I'm willing to show the meaning of
what has just now happened to me. You see, gentlemen of the jury—
for in calling *you* "jurors" I no doubt use the term correctly—an
amazing thing has happened to me. In previous times, the usual
5   prophecies of my daimonic sign were always very frequent, opposing
me even on trivial matters, if I was about do something that wasn't
right. Now, however, something has happened to me, as you can see
for yourselves, that one might think to be, and that's generally
regarded as being, the worst of all bad things. Yet the god's sign didn't
40b   oppose me when I left home this morning, or when I came up here
to the law court, or anywhere in my speech when I was about to say
something, even though in other discussions it has often stopped me
in the middle of what I was saying. Now, however, where this affair is
5   concerned, it has opposed me in nothing I either said or did.
What, then, do I suppose is the explanation for that? I'll tell you.
You see, it's likely that what has happened to me is a good thing and
that those of you who suppose death to be bad make an incorrect
40c   supposition. I've strong evidence of this, since there's no way my
usual sign would have failed to oppose me, if I weren't about to
achieve something good.
But let's bear in mind that the following is also a strong reason to
5   hope that death may be something good. Being dead is one of two
things: either the dead are nothing, as it were, and have no awareness
whatsoever of anything at all; or else, as we're told, it's some sort of
change, a migration of the soul from here to another place. Now, if
there's in fact no awareness, but it's like sleep—the kind in which the
40d   sleeper has no dream whatsoever—then death would be an amazing
advantage. For I imagine that if someone had to pick a night in which
he slept so soundly that he didn't even dream and had to compare all
5   the other nights and days of his life with that one, and then, having
considered the matter, had to say how many days or nights of his life
he had spent better or more pleasantly than that night—I imagine

that not just some private individual, but even the great king,[104] would find them easy to count compared to the other days and nights. Well, if death's like that, *I* say it's an advantage, since, in that case, the whole of time would seem no longer than a single night.   40e

On the other hand, if death's a sort of journey from here to another place, and if what we're told is true, and all who've died are indeed there, what could be a greater good than that, gentlemen of the jury? If on arriving in Hades and leaving behind the people who claim to be jurors here, one's going to find those who are truly jurors or judges, the very ones who are said to sit in judgment there too—Minos, Rhadamanthys, Aeachus, Triptolemus,[105] and all the other demigods who were just in their own lifetimes—would the journey be a wretched one?   41a

5

5

Or again, what would any one of you not give to talk to Orpheus and Museus, Hesiod and Homer?[106] I'd be willing to die many times over, if that were true. You see, for myself, at any rate, spending time there would be amazing: when I met Palamedes[107] or Ajax, the son of Telemon,[108] or anyone else of old who died because of an unjust   41b

---

104. The king of Persia, whose wealth and power made him a popular exemplar of human success and happiness (*Gorgias* 470e4–9; *Euthydemus* 274a6–7; *Sophist* 230d8–e3; *Laws* 693d1–696a4).

105. Minos was a legendary king of Crete. He judges among the dead in Hades as he did among the living—though not for wrongs they committed in this life. Rhadamanthys is usually thought to judge not in Hades but in the Isles of the Blessed. Aeachus is the judge and lawgiver of Aegina and an arbiter among the gods. Triptolemus, a hero from Eleusis, had a prominent role in mystery cults.

106. Orpheus was a legendary bard and founder of the mystical religion of Orphism. Museus, usually associated with Orpheus, was also a legendary bard. Hesiod, an early Greek poet, is the author of *Theogony* (a work on the genealogy of the gods) and *Works and Days* (a work of practical advice and moral suasion). Homer, the greatest Greek epic poet, is the author of the *Iliad* (which deals with events in the war between the Greeks and the Trojans) and the *Odyssey* (which deals with the adventures of Odysseus [41c1 note] during his journey home from the Trojan War).

107. Aeschylus, Sophocles, and Euripides all wrote tragedies named after him, and Gorgias (19e3 note) wrote a defense of him. Odysseus (41c1 note) hid gold in his tent, forged a letter that compromised him, accused him of treason, and had him stoned to death.

108. Ajax was cheated of the armor of Achilles in competition with Odysseus (41c1 note). Driven mad, as a result of this injustice, he committed suicide. Sophocles' *Ajax* deals with these events.

verdict, I could compare my own experience with theirs—as I suppose it wouldn't be unpleasing to do. And in particular, the most
5   important thing: I could spend time examining and searching people there, just as I do here, to find out who among them is wise, and who thinks he is, but isn't.

What wouldn't one give, gentlemen of the jury, to be able to examine the leader of the great expedition against Troy,[109] or Odys-
41c   seus,[110] or Sisyphus,[111] or countless other men and women one could mention? To talk to them there, to associate with them and examine them, wouldn't that be inconceivable happiness? In any case, the peo-
5   ple there certainly don't kill one for doing it. For if what we're told is true, the people there are both happier in all other respects than the people here and also deathless for the remainder of time.

But you too, gentlemen of the jury, should be of good hope in the face of death, and bear in mind this single truth: nothing bad can
41d   happen to a good man, whether in life or in death, nor are the gods unconcerned about his troubles. What has happened to me hasn't happened by chance; rather, it's clear to me that to die now and escape my troubles was a better thing for me. It was for this very rea-
5   son that my sign never opposed me. And so, for my part, I'm not at all angry with those who voted to condemn me or with my accusers. And yet this wasn't what they had in mind when they were condemning and accusing me. No, they thought to harm me—and for that they deserve to be blamed.

41e   This small favor, however, I ask of them.[112] When my sons come of age, gentlemen, punish them by harassing them in the very same way that I harassed you, if they seem to you to take care of wealth or
5   anything before virtue, if they think they're someone when they're no one. Reproach them, just as I reproached you: tell them that they don't care for the things they should and think they're someone when

---

109. Agamemnon, king of Mycenae.

110. Odysseus is a legendary hero of the Trojan War, prominent in Homer's *Iliad* and central to his *Odyssey*. He was as famous for his cunning as for his skill in battle.

111. Sisyphus is a legendary king and founder of Corinth. A trickster who tried to cheat death, he was punished in Hades by having to roll a boulder to the top of a hill, only to have to do so over and over again, since it always rolled back down. A spurious work in the Platonic canon is named after him.

112. Not just the jurors who voted to condemn Socrates, presumably, but as "gentlemen" in the next sentence suggests, the entire jury.

they're worth nothing. If you will do that, I'll have received my own 42a
just deserts from you, as will my sons.

But now it's time to leave, I to die and you to live. Which of us goes
to the better thing, however, is unclear to everyone except the god. 5

CRITO

SOCRATES: Why have you come at this hour, Crito? Isn't it still
43a early?

CRITO:[1] It is indeed.

SOCRATES: About what time?

CRITO: Just before dawn.

5 SOCRATES: I'm surprised the prison warden was willing to let
you in.

CRITO: He knows me by now, Socrates, I come here so often.
And besides I've done him a good turn.

SOCRATES: Have you just arrived or have you been here for a
while?

10 CRITO: For quite a while.

43b SOCRATES: Then why didn't you wake me right away, instead of
sitting there in silence?

CRITO: In the name of Zeus, Socrates, I wouldn't do that! I only
wish I weren't so sleepless and distressed myself. I've been amazed
5 all this time to see how peacefully you were sleeping, and I deliberately kept from waking you, so that you could pass the time as
pleasantly as possible. In the past—indeed, throughout my entire
life—I've often counted you happy in your disposition, but never
more so than in this present misfortune. You bear it so easily and
calmly.

SOCRATES: Well, Crito, it would be an error for someone of my
10 age to complain when the time has come when he must die.

43c CRITO: Other people get overtaken by such misfortunes too,
Socrates, but their age doesn't prevent them in the least from com-
plaining about their fate.

SOCRATES: That's right. But tell me, why *have* you come so early?

5 CRITO: I bring bad news, Socrates. Not bad in your view, it seems
to me, but bad and hard in mine and that of all your friends—and
hardest of all, I think, for me to bear.

---

1. See *Apology* 33e1 note.

SOCRATES: What news is that? Or has the ship returned from Delos, at whose return I must die?[2]   43d

CRITO: No, it hasn't returned *yet*, but I think it will arrive today, judging from the reports of people who've come from Sunium,[3] where they left it. It's clear from these reports that it will arrive today. And so tomorrow, Socrates, you must end your life.   5

SOCRATES: I pray that it may be for the best, Crito. If it pleases the gods, let it be so. All the same, I don't think it will arrive today.

CRITO: What evidence have you for that?   44a

SOCRATES: I'll tell you. I must die on the day after the ship arrives.

CRITO: That's what the authorities[4] say, at least.

SOCRATES: Then I don't think it will arrive today, but tomorrow. My   5
evidence for this comes from a dream I had in the night a short while ago. So it looks as though you chose the right time not to wake me.

CRITO: What was your dream?

SOCRATES: I thought a beautiful, graceful woman came to me,   10
robed in white. She called me and said, "Socrates, you will arrive 'in   44b
fertile Phthia' on the third day."[5]

CRITO: What a strange dream, Socrates.

---

2. Legend had it that Athens was once obliged to send King Minos of Crete an annual tribute of seven young men and seven maidens to be given to the Minotaur—a monster, half man and half bull, that he kept in a labyrinth. With the help of a thread given to him by Minos' daughter Ariadne, Theseus, a legendary king of Athens, made his way through the labyrinth, killed the Minotaur, and escaped, thus ending the tribute. Each year, Athens commemorated these events by sending a mission of thanks to the sanctuary of Apollo on the sacred island of Delos. No executions could take place in Athens until it returned from its voyage. See *Phaedo* 58a3–c5.

3. A headland on the southeast coast of Attica, about 30 miles from Athens.

4. Namely, the Eleven. See *Apology* 37c2 note.

5. The quotation is from Homer, *Iliad* IX.363. Agamemnon (*Apology* 41c1), leader of the Greek forces, has insulted Achilles (*Apology* 28c4 note) by taking back his war prize, Briseis. Achilles withdraws from the battle, so that the Greeks suffer terrible losses. Agamemnon, realizing his mistake, offers enormous recompense but without coming to apologize in person. In response, Achilles threatens to set sail the next morning, so that with good weather he will arrive at his home "in fertile Phthia" on the third day. The dream means that Socrates' soul will find its home on the third day (counting, as usual among the Greeks, both the first and last member of the series).

SOCRATES: Yet its meaning is quite clear, Crito—at least, it seems
5 so to me.

CRITO: All too clear, apparently. But look here, Socrates, it's still
not too late to take my advice and save yourself. You see, if you die, I
won't just suffer a single misfortune. On the contrary, not only will I
lose a friend the like of whom I'll never find again, but, in addition,
10 many people, who don't know you or me well, will think that I
didn't care about you, since I could have saved you if I'd been willing
44c to spend the money. And indeed what reputation could be more
shameful than being thought to value money more than friends? For
the majority of people won't believe that it was you yourself who
5 refused to leave this place, though we were urging you to do so.

SOCRATES: But my dear Crito, why should we care so much
about what the majority think? After all, the most decent ones, who
are worthier of consideration, will believe that matters were handled
in just the way they were in fact handled.

44d CRITO: But you can surely see, Socrates, that one should care
about majority opinion too. Your present situation itself shows clearly
that the majority can do not just minor harms but the very worst
5 things to someone who's been slandered in front of them.

SOCRATES: I only wish, Crito, that the majority *could* do the very
worst things, then they might also be able to do the very best ones—
and everything would be fine. But as it is, they can do neither, since
they can't make someone either wise or unwise—the effects *they* pro-
10 duce are really the result of chance.[6]

44e CRITO: Well, if you say so. But tell me this, Socrates. You're not
worried about me and your other friends, are you—fearing that if
you escaped, the informers[7] would give us trouble, and that we might
5 be forced to give up all our property, pay heavy fines, or even suffer
some further penalty? If you're afraid of anything like that, dismiss it
45a from your mind. After all, we're surely justified in running this risk to

---

6. Socrates often argues that wisdom is the only really good thing and ignorance
(lack of wisdom) the only really bad one. See *Charmides* 174b11–c3; *Euthydemus*
281d2–e5; *Meno* 87d2–89a5. Because the majority are unwise, they cannot reliably produce the effects they want.

7. *Sukophantai*: individuals who prosecuted others in order to get the reward offered in Athenian law to successful prosecutors as public benefactors, or as a way
of blackmailing someone who would pay to avoid prosecution, or for personal or
political gain of some other sort.

save you or an even greater one if need be. Now take my advice, and don't refuse me.

SOCRATES: Yes, those things do worry me, Crito, among many others.

CRITO: Then don't fear them: the sum of money that certain people I know will accept in order to save you and get you out of here isn't that large. Next, don't you see how cheap these informers are and how little money is needed to deal with them? My own wealth's available to you, and it, I think, should be enough. Next, even if your concern for me makes you unwilling to spend my money, there are foreign visitors here who are willing to spend theirs. One of them, Simmias of Thebes, has even brought enough money for this very purpose; and Cebes, too, and a good many others are also willing to contribute.[8] So, as I say, don't let these fears make you hesitate to save yourself. And don't let it trouble you, as you were saying in court, that if you went into exile you wouldn't know what to do with yourself.[9] You see, wherever else you may go, there'll be people to welcome you. If you want to go to Thessaly, I have friends there who'll make much of you and protect you, so that no one in Thessaly will give you any trouble.[10]

Besides, Socrates, I think that what you're doing isn't just: throwing away your life, when you could save it, and hastening the very sort of fate for yourself that your enemies would hasten—and indeed have hastened—in their wish to destroy you. What's more I think you're also betraying those sons of yours[11] by going away and deserting them when you could bring them up and educate them. So far as you're concerned, they must take their chances in life; and the chance they'll get, in all likelihood, is just the one that orphans usually get when they lose their parents.[12] No. Either one shouldn't have

45b

5

45c

5

10

45d

---

8. Simmias and Cebes (also from Thebes) were followers of Socrates and serve as his chief interlocutors in *Phaedo*.

9. See *Apology* 37c4–e2.

10. Thessaly is a region in the north of Greece.

11. See *Apology* 34d6–8.

12. See Homer, *Iliad* XXII.490–498: "An orphan has no friends. / He hangs his head, his cheeks are wet with tears. / He has to beg from his dead father's friends, / Tugging on one man's cloak, another's tunic, / And if they pity him he gets to sip / From someone's cup, just enough to moisten / His lips but not enough to quench his thirst. / Or a child with both parents still alive / Will push him away from a feast, taunting him, / 'Go away, your father doesn't eat with us.'" (Trans. Stanley Lombardo.)

5   children at all, or one ought to see their upbringing and education
through to the end. But you seem to me to be choosing the easiest
way out, whereas one should choose whatever a good and brave man
would choose—particularly when one claims to have cared about
virtue throughout one's life.[13]

      I feel ashamed on your behalf and on behalf of myself and your
45e   friends. I fear that it's going to seem that this whole business of yours
has been handled with a certain cowardice on our part. The case was
brought to court when it needn't have been brought.[14] Then there
was the actual conduct of the trial. And now, to crown it all, this
5   absurd finale to the affair. It's going to seem that we let the opportunity slip because of some vice, such as cowardice, on our part, since
46a   we didn't save you nor did you save yourself, although it was quite
possible had we been of even the slightest use.

      See to it, then, Socrates, that all this doesn't turn out badly and a
shameful thing both for you and for us. Come, deliberate—or
rather, at this hour it's not a matter of deliberating but of having
5   deliberated already—and only one decision remains. You see, everything must be done this coming night; and if we delay, it will no
longer be possible. For all these reasons, Socrates, please take my
advice and don't refuse me.

46b   SOCRATES: My dear Crito, your enthusiasm's most valuable, provided it's of the right sort. But if it isn't, the greater it is, the more difficult it will be to deal with. We must therefore examine whether we
should do what you advise or not. You see, I'm not the sort of person
who's just now for the first time persuaded by nothing within me
5   except the argument that on rational reflection seems best to me;[15]
I've *always* been like that. I can't now reject the arguments I stated
before just because this misfortune has befallen me. On the contrary,
they seem pretty much the same to me, and I respect and value the
46c   same ones as I did before. So if we have no better ones to offer in the
present situation, you can be sure I won't agree with you—not even if
the power of the majority to threaten us, as if we were children, with
5   the bogeymen of imprisonment, execution, and confiscation of property were far greater than it is now.

---

13. See *Apology* 32c8–33a5.

14. See *Apology* 29c2 and note.

15. See *Euthyphro* 14e9.

What, then, is the most reasonable way to examine these matters? Suppose we first take up the argument you stated about people's opinions. Is it true or not that one should pay attention to some opinions but not to others? Or was it true before I had to die, whereas it's now clear that it was stated idly, for the sake of argument, and is really just childish nonsense? For my part, I'm eager to join you, Crito, in a joint examination of whether this argument will appear any differently to me, now that I'm here, or the same, and of whether we should dismiss it from our minds or be persuaded by it. 46d 5

It used to be said, I think, by people who thought they were talking sense, that, as I said a moment ago, one should take some people's opinions seriously but not others. By the gods, Crito, don't you think that was true? You see, in all human probability, *you* are not going to die tomorrow, and so the present situation won't distort your judgment. Consider, then, don't you think it's a sound argument that one shouldn't value all the opinions people have, but some and not others, and not those of everyone, but those of some people and not of others? What do you say? Isn't that true? 46e 47a 5

CRITO: It is.

SOCRATES: And we should value good opinions, but not bad ones?

CRITO: Yes.

SOCRATES: And the good ones are those of wise people and the bad ones those of unwise people? 10

CRITO: Of course.

SOCRATES: Come then, what of such questions as this? When a man's primarily engaged in physical training, does he pay attention to the praise or blame or opinion of every man or only to those of the one man who's a doctor or a trainer? 47b

CRITO: Only to those of the one man.

SOCRATES: Then he should fear the blame and welcome the praise of that one man, but not those of the majority of people. 5

CRITO: Clearly.

SOCRATES: So his actions and exercises, his eating and drinking, should be guided by the opinion of the one man, the knowledgeable and understanding supervisor, rather than on that of all the rest? 10

CRITO: That's right.

SOCRATES: Well, then, if he disobeys that one man and sets no
47c value on his opinion or his praises but values those of the majority of
people who have no understanding, won't something bad happen to
him?

CRITO: Of course.

SOCRATES: And what is this bad effect? Where does it occur? In
what part of the one who disobeys?

CRITO: Clearly, it's in his body, since that's what it destroys.

SOCRATES: That's right. And isn't the same true in other cases,
Crito? No need to go through them all, but, in particular, in cases of
just and unjust things, shameful and fine ones, good and bad ones—in
cases of what we're now deliberating about—is it the opinion of the
47d majority we should follow and fear? Or is it the opinion of the one
man—if there is one who understands these things—we should
respect and fear above all others? On the grounds that, if we don't follow it, we shall seriously damage and maim that part of us which, as
we used to say, is made better by what's just but is destroyed by what's
5 unjust. Or is there no truth in that?

CRITO: I certainly think there is, Socrates.

SOCRATES: Come then, suppose we destroy the part of us that is
made better by what's healthy but is seriously damaged by what
causes disease when we don't follow the opinion of people who have
10 understanding. Would our lives be worth living once it has been seri-
47e ously damaged?[16] And that part, of course, is the body, isn't it?

CRITO: Yes.

SOCRATES: Then are our lives worth living with a wretched, seri-
5 ously damaged body?

CRITO: Certainly not.

SOCRATES: But our lives *are* worth living when the part of us
that's maimed by what's unjust and benefited by what's just is seriously damaged? Or do we consider it—whichever part of us it is to
48a which justice and injustice pertain—to be inferior to the body?

CRITO: Certainly not.

SOCRATES: On the contrary, it's more valuable?

CRITO: Far more.

---

16. See *Apology* 38a5–6.

SOCRATES: Then, my very good friend, we should not give so much thought to what the majority of people will say about us, but think instead of what the person who understands just and unjust things will say—the one man and the truth itself. So your first claim—that we should give thought to the opinion of the majority about what's just, fine, good, and their opposites—isn't right.

"But," someone might say, "the majority can put us to death."

CRITO: That's certainly clear too. It would indeed be said, Socrates.

SOCRATES: That's right. And yet, my dear friend, the argument we've gone through still seems the same to me, at any rate, as it did before. And now examine this further one to see whether we think it still stands[17] or not: the most important thing isn't living, but living well.

CRITO: Yes, it still stands.

SOCRATES: And the argument that living well, living a fine life, and living justly are the same[18]—does it still stand or not?

CRITO: It still stands.

SOCRATES: Then in the light of these agreements, we should examine whether or not it would be just for me to try to get out of here when the Athenians haven't acquitted me. And if it does seem just, we should make the attempt, and if it doesn't, we should abandon the effort.

As for those other considerations you raise about loss of money and people's opinions and bringing up children—they, in truth, Crito, are appropriate considerations for people who readily put one to death and would as readily bring one back to life again if they could, without thinking; I mean, the majority of people. For us, however, the argument has made the decision. There's nothing else to be examined besides the very thing we just mentioned: whether we—both the ones who are rescued and also the rescuers themselves—will be acting justly if we pay money to those who would get me out of here and do them favors, or whether we will in truth be acting unjustly if we do those things. And if it appears that we will be acting unjustly in doing them, we have no need at all to give any opposing weight to our having to

5

10

48b

5

48c

5

48d

---

17. Or stays put. See *Euthyphro* 11b6–e1.
18. So that living justly guarantees (or is the same thing as) living a happy life.

die—or suffer in some other way—if we stay here and mind our
5 behavior when the alternative is doing injustice.[19]

CRITO: What you *say* seems true to me, Socrates. But I wish you'd consider what we're to *do*.

SOCRATES: Let's examine that question together, my dear friend, and if you can oppose anything I say, oppose it, and I'll be persuaded
48e by you. But if you can't, be a good fellow and stop telling me the same thing over and over, that I should leave here against the will of the Athenians. You see, I think it very important that I act in this matter having persuaded you, rather than against your will. Consider,
5 then, the starting point of our inquiry, to see if you find it adequately
49a formulated, and try to answer my questions as you really think best.

CRITO: I'll certainly try.

SOCRATES: Do we say that one should never do injustice intentionally? Or may injustice be done in some circumstances but not in
5 others? Is doing injustice never good or fine, as we have often agreed in the past? Or have all these former agreements been discarded during these last few days? Can you and I at our age, Crito, have spent so
10 long in serious discussion with one another without realizing that we
49b ourselves were no better than a pair of children? Or is what we used to say true above all else: that whether the majority of people agree or not, and whether we must suffer still worse things than at present or ones that are easier to bear, it's true, all the same, that doing injustice in any circumstances is bad and shameful for the one who does it? Is
5 that what we say or not?

CRITO: It is what we say.

SOCRATES: So one should never do injustice.

CRITO: Certainly not.

SOCRATES: So one shouldn't do injustice in return for injustice, as the majority of people think—seeing that one should *never* do
10 injustice.

49c CRITO: Apparently not.

SOCRATES: Well then, should one do wrong or not?

CRITO: Certainly not, Socrates.

---

19. This doctrine—that faced with a choice between acting unjustly and *anything else whatever*, one must choose the latter—is Socrates' supreme principle of practical choice. See *Apology* 28b5–9, d6–10.

SOCRATES: Well, what about when someone does wrong in return for having suffered wrongdoing? Is that just, as the majority of people think, or not just? 5

CRITO: It's not just at all.

SOCRATES: No, for there's no difference, I take it, between doing wrong and doing injustice?

CRITO: That's right.

SOCRATES: So one must neither do injustice in return nor wrong any man, no matter what one has suffered at his hands. And, Crito, in 10 agreeing to this, watch out that you're not agreeing to anything contrary to what you believe. You see, I know that only a few people do 49d believe or will believe it. And between those who believe it and those who don't, there's no common basis for deliberation, but each necessarily regards the other with contempt when they see their deliberations. You too, then, should consider very carefully whether you share 5 that belief with me and whether the following is the starting point of our deliberations: that it's never right to do injustice, or to do injustice in return, or to retaliate with bad treatment when one has been treated badly.[20] Or do you disagree and not share this starting point? You see, I've believed this for a long time myself and still believe it now. But if 49e you've come to some other opinion, say so. Instruct me. If you stand by the former one, however, then listen to my next point.

CRITO: Yes, I do stand by it and share it with you, so go on.

SOCRATES: Then I'll state the next point—or rather, ask a question: should one do the things one has agreed with someone to do, 5 provided they are just, or should one cheat?

CRITO: One should do them.

SOCRATES: Then consider what follows. If we leave this place without having persuaded the city, are we treating some people badly—and those whom we should least of all treat in that way—or 50a not? Are we standing by agreements that are just or not?

CRITO: I can't answer your question, Socrates, since I don't understand it. 5

---

20. This abandonment of the conventional doctrine that justice consists in "doing good to friends and harm to enemies" (*Meno* 71e1–5), that retaliation is a fundamental principle of justice, is one of Socrates' most revolutionary moral doctrines, as he himself recognizes here.

SOCRATES: Well, look at it this way. Suppose we were about to run away from here—or whatever what we'd be doing should be called.[21] And suppose the Laws and the city community came and confronted us, and said,

50b   "Tell us, Socrates, what do you intend to do? Do you intend anything else by this act you're attempting than to destroy us Laws, and the city as a whole, to the extent that you can? Or do you think that a city can continue to exist and not be overthrown if the legal judgments rendered in it have no force, but are deprived of authority and undermined by the actions of private individuals?"

5   What shall we say in response to that question, Crito, and to others like it? For there's a lot that one might say—particularly, if one were an orator—on behalf of this law we're destroying, the one requiring that legal judgments, once rendered, have authority. Or shall we say to

50c   them, "Yes, that's what we intend, for the city treated us unjustly and didn't judge our lawsuit correctly." Is that what we're to say—or what?

CRITO: Yes, by Zeus, that's what we're to say, Socrates.

5   SOCRATES: Then what if the Laws replied, "Was that also part of the agreement between you and us, Socrates? Or did you agree to stand by whatever judgments the city rendered?" Then, if we were surprised at the words, perhaps they might say, "Don't be surprised at what we're saying, Socrates, but answer us—since you're so accus-

10   tomed to using question and answer. Come now, what charge have you to bring against the city and ourselves that you should try to

50d   destroy us? In the first place, wasn't it we who gave you birth—wasn't it through us that your father married your mother and produced you? Tell us, do you have some complaint about the correctness of those of us Laws concerned with marriage?"

"No, I have no complaint," I'd reply.

5   "Well then, what about the Laws dealing with the bringing up and educating of children, under which you were educated yourself? Didn't those of us Laws who regulate that area prescribe correctly when we ordered your father to educate you in the arts and physical training?"[22]

"They prescribed correctly," I'd reply.

---

21. See *Apology* 28d5–29c1, 38e5–39b1.

22. *Mousikē* and *gymnastikē*: traditional Greek education in poetry, song, and music, on the one hand, and dancing, physical training, and preparatory military training, on the other.

"Good. Then since you were born, brought up, and educated, can 50e
you deny, first, that you're our offspring and slave, both yourself and
your ancestors? And if that's so, do you think that what's just is based
on an equality between you and us, that whatever we try to do to you 5
it's just for you to do to us in return? As regards you and your father (or
you and your master, if you happened to have one), what's just isn't
based on equality, and so you don't return whatever treatment you
receive—answering back when you're criticized or striking back when
you're struck, or doing many other such things. As regards you and 51a
your fatherland and its Laws, then, are these things permitted? If we try
to destroy you, believing it to be just, will you try to destroy us Laws
and your fatherland, to the extent that you can? And will you claim 5
that you're acting justly in doing so—you the man who really cares
about virtue? Or are you so wise that it has escaped your notice that
your fatherland is more worthy of honor than your mother and father
and all your other ancestors; that it is more to be revered and more
sacred and is held in greater esteem both among the gods and among 51b
those human beings who have any sense; that you must treat your
fatherland with piety, submitting to it and placating it more than you
would your own father when it is angry; that you must either persuade
it or else do whatever it commands; that you must mind your behavior 5
and undergo whatever treatment it prescribes for you, whether a beating or imprisonment; that if it leads you to war to be wounded or
killed, that's what you must do, and that's what is just—not to give way
or retreat or leave where you were stationed, but, on the contrary, in
war and law courts, and everywhere else, to do whatever your city or
fatherland commands or else persuade it as to what is really just;[23] and 10

---

23. The Laws say that *they* are to be persuaded—an obvious metaphor, made possible by their personification. They do not tell us how the metaphor is to be cashed
by identifying which of their representative bodies in Athens—the one that makes
the laws or the one that implements them—is the appropriate one to hear persua-
sion or specify the kind of alleged injustice it is appropriate to persuade about—
unjust laws, unjust judgments, or unjust sentences. They do say, however, that if
Socrates escapes execution, he *neither* persuades *nor* obeys. What he fails to obey is
presumably some law or laws. Only two have any bearing on his situation: (1) The
law against impiety under which he was indicted, and (2) the law on court judgments, which required him to abide by the decision of the court and not to try to
prevent its sentence from being carried out (50a8–b5). Since the only one of these
that Socrates wouldn't obey by escaping is (2), what the Laws are asserting seems
to be this: (A) *A citizen of Athens who has broken, or been accused of breaking, one of its*

51c   that while it is impious to violate the will of your mother or father, it is
       yet less so than to violate that of your fatherland."

       What are we to say to that, Crito? Are the Laws telling the truth or
       not?

5   CRITO: Yes, I think they are.

       SOCRATES: "Consider, then, Socrates," the Laws might perhaps
       continue, "whether we're also telling the truth in saying this: that you
       aren't treating us justly in what you're now trying to do. You see, we
       gave you birth, upbringing, and education, and have provided you, as
       well as every other citizen, with a share of all the fine things we
51d   could. Nonetheless, if any Athenian—who has been admitted to adult
       status and has observed both how affairs are handled in the city and
       ourselves, the Laws—is dissatisfied with us and wishes to leave, we
5   grant him permission to take his property and go wherever he pleases.
       Not one of us Laws stands in his way or forbids it. If any one of you is
       dissatisfied with us and the city and wishes to go to a colony or to live
       as an alien elsewhere,[24] he may go wherever he wishes and hold on to
51e   what's his.

       "*But* if any of you stays here, after he has observed the way we
       judge lawsuits and the other ways in which we manage the city, then
       we say that he has agreed with us by his action to do whatever we
5   command. And we say that whoever does not obey commits a three-
       fold injustice: he disobeys us as his parents; he disobeys us as those
       who brought him up; and, after having agreed to obey us, he neither

       ---

       laws must, if summoned, either persuade a court that he has done nothing unjust or abide
       by the court's judgment and obey the law requiring him to submit to the sentence passed on
       him. That is why the Laws don't "harshly command" (52a1) Socrates; they give
       him the option of defending himself before a jury. But if he doesn't succeed in
       persuading the jury of his innocence, he must obey, not (1) the law he has already
       allegedly broken (that would make little sense), but (2). If, however, the sentence
       chosen by the jury requires Socrates to do something unjust—for example, to stop
       philosophizing—he will disobey it (*Apology* 29b9–d5). But he would violate (A)
       in doing so only if, having been called before a court to account for his disobedi-
       ence, and having failed to persuade it that his disobedience was just, he tried to
       escape the sentence it imposed.

       24. When the population of a Greek city became too large for its available re-
       sources, it often sent some of its citizens out to found a new city elsewhere. This
       so-called colony (*apoikia*) was politically autonomous but typically retained some
       significant ties with its mother city. For example, its citizens were not resident
       aliens when living in the new city.

obeys nor persuades us, if we're doing something that isn't right. Yet we offer him a choice and do not harshly command him to do what he's told. On the contrary, we offer two alternatives: he must either **52a** persuade us or do what we say. And he does neither. These, then, are the charges, Socrates, to which we say you too will become liable, if you do what you have in mind—and you won't be among the least liable of the Athenians, but among the most." 5

Then, if I were to say, "Why is that?" perhaps they might justifiably reproach me by saying that I am among the Athenians who have made that agreement with them in the strongest terms.

"Socrates," they would say, "we have the strongest evidence that **52b** you were satisfied with us and with the city. After all, you'd never have stayed at home here so much more consistently than all the rest of the Athenians if you weren't also much more consistently satisfied. You never left the city for a festival, except once to go to the Isth- 5 mus.[25] You never went anywhere else, except for military service.[26] You never went abroad as other people do. You had no desire to acquaint yourself with other cities or other laws. On the contrary, we and our city sufficed for you. So emphatically did you choose us and **52c** agree to live as a citizen under us, that you even produced children here. *That's* how satisfied you were with the city.

"Moreover, even at your very trial, you could have proposed exile as a counterpenalty if you'd wished, and what you're now trying to do against the city's will, you could then have done with its consent.[27] 5 On that occasion, you prided yourself on not feeling resentful that you had to die.[28] You'd choose death before exile—so you said. Now, however, you feel no shame at those words and show no regard for us Laws as you try to destroy us. You're acting exactly the way the most wretched slave would act by trying to run away, contrary to your **52d** commitments and your agreements to live as a citizen under us.

"First, then, answer us on this very point: are we telling the truth when we say that you agreed, by deeds not words, to live as a citizen 5 under us? Or is that untrue?"

---

25. The narrow strip of land connecting the Peloponnese to the rest of Greece, where the Isthmian Games were held.

26. See *Apology* 28e1–3 and note.

27. See *Apology* 34d9 note.

28. See *Apology* 41d6–7.

What are we to reply to that, Crito? Mustn't we agree?

CRITO: We must, Socrates.

SOCRATES: "Well then," they might say, "surely you're breaking the commitments and agreements you made with us. You weren't coerced or tricked into agreeing or forced to decide in a hurry. On the contrary, you had seventy years in which you could have left if you weren't satisfied with us or if you thought those agreements unjust. You, however, preferred neither Sparta nor Crete—places you often say have good law and order[29]—nor any other Greek or foreign city. On the contrary, you went abroad less often than the lame, the blind, or other handicapped people. Hence it's clear that you, more than any other Athenian, have been consistently satisfied with your city and with us Laws—for who would be satisfied by a city but not by its laws? Won't you, then, stand by your agreements now? Yes, you will, if you're persuaded by us, Socrates, and at least you won't make yourself a laughingstock by leaving the city.

"For consider now: if you break those agreements, if you commit any of these wrongs, what good will you do yourself or your friends? You see, it's pretty clear that your friends will risk being exiled themselves as well as being disenfranchised and having their property confiscated. As for you, if you go to one of the nearest cities, Thebes or Megara—for they both have good laws—you will be arriving there, Socrates, as an enemy of their political systems, and those who care about their own cities will look on you with suspicion, regarding you as one who undermines laws. You will also confirm your jurors in their opinion, so that they will think they judged your lawsuit correctly. For anyone who undermines laws might very well be considered a corruptor of young and ignorant people.

"Will you, then, avoid cities with good law and order, and men of the most respectable kind? And if so, will your life be worth living? Or will you associate with these people and be shameless enough to converse with them? And what will you say, Socrates? The very things that you said here, about how virtue and justice are man's most valuable possessions, along with law and lawful conduct. Don't you think Socrates and everything about him will look unseemly? Surely, you must.

"Or will you keep away from those places and go to Crito's friends in Thessaly? After all, there's complete disorder and laxity there, so

52e
5
53a
5

10
53b
5
53c
5
53d

---

29. *Eunomia*: good laws and compliance with them.

perhaps they'd enjoy hearing about your absurd escape from prison
when you dressed up in disguise, wore a peasant's leather jerkin or   5
some other such escapee's outfit, and altered your appearance. And
will no one remark on the fact that you, an old man, with probably
only a short time left to live, were so greedy for life that you dared to   53e
violate the most important laws?[30] Perhaps not, provided you don't
annoy anyone. Otherwise, you'll hear many disparaging things said
about you. Will you live by currying favor with every man and acting
the slave—and do nothing in Thessaly besides eat, as if you'd gone to   5
live in Thessaly for a good dinner? As for those arguments about justice and the rest of virtue, where, tell us, will they be?   54a

"Is it that you want to live for your children's sake, then, to bring
them up and educate them? Really? Will you bring them up and educate them by taking them to Thessaly and making foreigners of them,   5
so they can enjoy that privilege too? If not, will they be better
brought up and educated here without you, provided that you're still
alive? 'Of course,' you may say, because your friends will take care of
them. Then will they take care of them if you go to Thessaly, but not
take care of them if you go to Hades? If those who call themselves   10
your friends are worth anything at all, you surely can't believe that.   54b

"No, Socrates, be persuaded by us who reared you. Don't put a
higher value on children, on life, or on anything else than on what's
just, so that when you reach Hades you may have all this to offer as   5
your defense before the authorities there. For if you do do that, it
doesn't seem that it will be better for you *here*, or for any of your
friends, or that it will be more just or more pious. And it won't be
better for you when you arrive *there* either. As it is, you'll leave here—
if you do leave—as one who has been treated unjustly not by us Laws,
but by men. But suppose you leave, suppose you return injustice for   54c
injustice and bad treatment for bad treatment in that shameful way,
breaking your agreements and commitments with us and doing bad
things to those whom you should least of all treat in that way—yourself, your friends, your fatherland, and ourselves. Then we'll be angry   5
with you while you're still alive, and our brothers, the Laws of Hades,
won't receive you kindly there, knowing that you tried to destroy us
to the extent you could. Come, then, don't let Crito persuade you to
follow his advice rather than ours."   54d

---

30. See *Phaedo* 117a1–3 below.

That, Crito, my dear friend, is what I seem to hear them saying, you may be sure. And, just like those Corybantes who think they are still hearing the flutes,[31] the echo of their arguments reverberates in me and makes me incapable of hearing anything else. No, as far as my present thoughts go, at least, you may be sure that if you argue against them, you will speak in vain. All the same, if you think you can do any more, please tell me.

CRITO: No, Socrates, I've nothing to say.

54e   SOCRATES: Then, let it be, Crito, and let's act in that way, since that's the way the god is leading us.

---

31. See *Apology* 27b6–7 and note. The Corybantes dance to the sound of flutes in the orgiastic rites of Dionysus—the god of wine and intoxication. Their music was supposed to induce a state of frenzied exhaustion in hysterical or emotionally disturbed people, from which they awoke relieved of their symptoms.

PHAEDO DEATH SCENE

(115b1–118a17)

A number of Socrates' friends have come to visit him in prison on the last day of his life. Their conversation focuses on the nature of the soul, arguments for its immortality, and the afterlife. We join it in its final stage. Phaedo—a close friend of Socrates from Elis in the Peloponnese—is the narrator.

"Well, Socrates," Crito said, "what are your final instructions for 115b these others or for me concerning your children or anything else? What can we do that would please you most?"

"Just the things I'm always saying, Crito," he said. "Nothing very new. If you take care of your own selves,[1] you'll please both me and 5 mine and yourselves in whatever you do—even if you make no agreements now. But if you don't take care of your own selves and are unwilling to live following the tracks, as it were, of our present and past discussions, then however much you may agree to do at this 10 moment, and however earnestly, you'll accomplish nothing." 115c

"We'll try hard, then, to do as you say," he said. "But how are we to bury you?"

"Whatever way you like," he said, "provided you can catch me, and I don't elude you." And laughing quietly and looking toward us, 5 he said, "Gentlemen, I can't persuade Crito that I am Socrates here, the one who's talking to you now and setting out in order each of the arguments put forward. He thinks I'm that corpse he'll see in a little while and actually asks how to bury me! As for the lengthy argument 115d I've been making, that when I drink the poison[2] I'll no longer stay put, but will take my leave of you and depart for certain happy conditions of the blessed—all that, I suppose, he regards as idle talk, intended to console all of you and myself as well. So I want you to 5 give a guarantee to Crito on my behalf," he said, "the opposite guarantee to the one he gave to the jurors.[3] His was that I'd stay put, whereas you must guarantee that I won't stay put when I die, but take

---

1. See *Apology* 29d2–30b4.
2. Executions in Athens were by poison hemlock.
3. See *Apology* 38a7–10.

115e   my leave of you and depart. In that way, Crito will bear it more easily
when he sees my body being burned or buried, and he won't feel
resentful on my behalf, as if I were suffering terrible things, and won't
say at the funeral that it's *Socrates* they're laying out, or bearing to the
grave, or burying. You see, you may be sure, my dearest Crito," he
said, "that false speaking is not only an error in its own terms, but also
does something bad to men's souls. No, you should be of good cheer,
and say you're burying *my body*, and bury it in any way you like and

116a   think most customary."

After saying that, he got up and went into another room to take
his bath.[4] Crito followed him, but he told us to stay where we were.
So we stayed there, talking among ourselves about what had been said
5   and reexamining it, and sometimes going over again how great a misfortune had befallen us. It was, we thought, simply as if we'd lost a
father and would spend the rest of our lives as orphans.[5]

When he had bathed and his children had been brought to him—
116b   two of his sons were small while one was older[6]—and those women
of his household[7] had come, he spoke with them in Crito's presence
and gave instructions as to his wishes. He then asked the women and
children to leave while he himself returned to us.

5   It was now almost sunset, since he'd spent a long time inside. He
came and sat down, fresh from his bath, and didn't talk much after
that. Then the agent of the Eleven[8] came and stood by him:
116c   "Socrates," he said, "I won't reproach you, as I reproach others, if
you're angry with me and curse me, when, on the orders of the officials, I tell you to drink the poison. During the rest of the time you've
5   spent here, I've known you as the most decent, gentlest, and best man
who's ever come to this place. And now, in particular, I'm sure that
you won't be angry with me, but with those whom you know to be
responsible. Now then, you know the message I've come to bring.
116d   Fare you well, and try to bear the inevitable as easily as you can." As
he said this, he burst into tears and turned to leave.

---

4. Socrates has said that he will bathe before taking the hemlock so as "to save the
women the trouble of washing the corpse" (115a8–9).

5. See *Crito* 45d3–4 and note.

6. See *Apology* 34d6–8.

7. Presumably his wife, Xanthippe, and others (60a3–5).

8. See *Apology* 37c2 and note.

Socrates looked up at him: "Fare you well too," he said, "we'll do
that." And turning to us, he said, "What a courteous fellow! During
the entire time I've been here he's come in and talked to me on occa-   5
sion, like the excellent man he is. And now how decent of him to
weep for me! Come then, Crito, let's do as he asks and have the poison brought if it's ready. If not, have the man prepare it."

"But Socrates," said Crito, "I think the sun's still on the mountains   116e
and hasn't yet set. What's more, I know that other people drink the
poison long after the order's been given, enjoying themselves with a
good dinner and plenty to drink and even, in some cases, by having
sex with whomever they happen to desire. Don't be in a hurry: 5
there's still time left."

And Socrates replied, "It's quite reasonable, Crito, for those people
to do those things, since they think they gain something by doing
them. And it's reasonable too for me not to do them, since I think I'll
gain nothing by drinking the poison a little later—apart, that is, from   117a
making myself look absurd in my own eyes by clinging greedily to life
and sparing the dregs.[9] Go on, now, do as I ask," he said, "and don't
refuse me."

Hearing this, Crito nodded to the slave who was standing nearby.   5
The slave went out and after a time returned with the man who was
going to administer the poison and was carrying it already mixed in a
cup. When Socrates saw the man, he said, "Well, my friend, you
know all about these things: what should I do?"   10

"Just drink it," he said, "and walk around until your legs feel
heavy; then lie down, and it will act of itself." With that, he handed   117b
Socrates the cup.

He took it quite calmly, Echecrates,[10] without a tremor or any
change of color or countenance; but giving the man his customary
mischievous stare, he said, "What do you say about pouring a libation   5
to someone from this drink? Is it permitted or not?"

"We prepare only as much as we think will be the sufficient dose,
Socrates," he said.

---

9. See Hesiod, *Works and Days* 368–369: "When the cask has just been opened,
and when it's almost gone, drink as much as you want; / Be sparing when it's half
full; but it's useless to spare the dregs." Also *Crito* 53d1–e2.

10. Echecrates, an adherent of Pythagorean philosophy, is the person to whom
Phaedo is narrating his account.

"I understand," he said. "But one is, I suppose, permitted to utter a
117c   prayer to the gods—and one should do so—that one's journey from
this world to the next will prove fortunate. That is my prayer; may it
be fulfilled." And with these words, he put the cup to his lips and
without the least difficulty or distaste drained it. Most of us had been
5   fairly well able to restrain our tears till then. But when we saw him
drinking it, and then that he had drunk it, we could do so no longer.
In my own case, the tears were pouring down my cheeks despite my
efforts, so that I covered my face and wept for myself—not for *him*,
certainly not, but for my own misfortune in losing such a man as a
117d   friend. Crito had got up and moved away even before I did, when he
was unable to hold back his tears. And Apollodorus,[11] who earlier still
had been weeping steadily, now burst forth in such a storm of tears
5   and distress that he made everyone present break down—except, that
is, for Socrates himself.

"What a way to behave, my friends!" he said. "Why it was for just
this reason, you know, that I sent the women away, so they wouldn't
commit these sorts of errors.[12] I've heard indeed that one should die in
117e   reverent silence. Come, mind your behavior and control yourselves."

When we heard this we were ashamed and checked our tears. He
walked around, and when his legs felt heavy, as he said, he lay down
5   on his back—as the man told him—and then the man, the one who'd
given him the poison, took hold of him[13] and after a while examined
his feet and legs. He then pinched his foot hard and asked if he could
feel it, and Socrates said, "No." After that, he did the same thing in
118a   turn to his shins; and moving upward in this way he showed us that
he was becoming cold and numb. He himself continued to keep hold
of him and said that when the coldness reached his heart, he'd be
5   gone.

Well, by this time the coldness was somewhere in the region of his
groin, when, uncovering his head—it had been covered up—he
spoke—and these were in fact the last words he uttered. "Crito," he

---

11. See *Apology* 34a2–3 note.

12. See 116b1–4.

13. Probably in order to steady Socrates during the convulsions that usually accom-
pany hemlock poisoning. Plato may have omitted more explicit reference to these
in order, among other things, to dramatize Socrates' tranquil acceptance of his fate.
See C. Gill, "The Death of Socrates," *Classical Quarterly* 23 (1973): 225–228.

said, "we owe a cock to Asclepius.[14] Please, don't forget to pay the debt."

"It shall be done," said Crito. "Is there anything else you want to say?"   10

To this question he gave no answer. But shortly afterward he stirred, and when the man uncovered him his eyes were fixed. Seeing this, Crito closed his mouth and his eyes.

Such was the end of our friend, Echecrates, a man who, we would   15
say, was the best of all those we've experienced and, generally speaking, the wisest and the most just.

---

14. Asclepius is the god of healing. The significance of Socrates' dying words has been much debated. See Glenn W. Most, "'A Cock for Asclepius,'" *Classical Quarterly* 43 (1993): 96–111.

ARISTOPHANES
Introduction

Aristophanes, the greatest of the Athenian comic playwrights, was born between 460 and 450 B.C.E. and died c. 386. Eleven of his perhaps as many as thirty plays survive together with almost a thousand fragments and citations.

The sort of comedy he wrote is not the sort with which we are familiar: situation comedy, comedy of errors and manners, plot and subplot, romance, with an emphasis on the familial and domestic. It's more like a dramatic combination of the slapstick of *The Three Stooges*, the song and dance of a Broadway musical, the verbal wit of a television show like *Frasier*, the open-ended plotline of *The Simpsons*, the parody of a Mel Brooks movie, the political satire of *Doonesbury*, and the outrageous sexuality of *The Rocky Horror Picture Show*, all wrapped up together in the format of a Monty Python movie.

The action of the comedy depends not on complicated plot or subtle interaction of characters, but on a bizarre idea (for example, the sex strike that stops the war in *Lysistrata*). The strategy is to wind up this idea, let it run, watch the logical (or illogical) conclusions that follow, and let the whole thing end in a great final scene. The creation and execution of the idea is the work of the play's central character. The backdrop is topical and immediate—the city of Athens in the present.[1]

The central character of our play, *Clouds*—first performed in 423 B.C.E., when Socrates was in his fifties—is Strepsiades. The bizarre idea is that of going to Socrates' school, the Pondertorium, in order to learn how to escape his creditors.

In the early verses of the play (112–118), Socrates appears: first, as the head of the Pondertorium, where, for a small fee, usually in kind (856–858, 1146–1149), one can learn the just logic, which represents traditional aristocratic values (961–1023), and also the unjust logic, which represents the new values of the sophists (1036–1104); second, as the ascetic high priest (833–839) of a mystery religion, with initiation rites (140), oaths of secrecy (143), and monastic seclusion (198–199), who teaches a variety of sciences, including a

---

1. I owe the foregoing description of Aristophanic comedy to Ian C. Storey. (*Aristophanes 1: Clouds, Wasps, Birds,* translated by Peter Meineck, Introduced by Ian C. Storey [Indianapolis: Hackett Publishing Company, 1998], p. vii.)

mechanistic theory of the cosmos (94–99, 331–407), on the basis of which he denies the existence of Zeus (367) and the other gods of tradition (423), worshipping in their place the various forms of Air (264), including the Clouds themselves (364).

Though each of these roles is important in the play, the first is more central to the plot than the second. For Strepsiades is not interested in mystery religion, science, or living in monastic seclusion. He comes to the Pondertorium, as we saw, solely for the purpose of learning the type of argument "that can argue a wrongful case and defeat the Superior Argument" (884) and help him escape the debts incurred by his extravagant son, Pheidippides (239–246). When Strepsiades turns out to be unteachable himself, he prevails on Pheidippides to attend the Pondertorium in his place.

Pheidippides proves more tractable than his father. He learns both the Superior and the Inferior Arguments and can defeat justice (887–888, 1339) with either one (1336–1337). But that means he can also defeat other traditional values, such as honoring parents, which his father, naturally enough, would like him to retain. The result is that Strepsiades blames Socrates for the corruption of his son (1464–1466) and burns the Pondertorium to the ground (1472–1510).

Socrates, the teacher of sophistical argument, is also crucial to the play for another reason. The vast majority of the specific scientific and related religious doctrines propounded in the Pondertorium have to do with air in some shape or form. And Air plays an integrative symbolic role in the play strongly at odds with its having an origin in anything other than Aristophanes' imagination. Air is the medium of speech. Therefore, Clouds, a form of air (330) both visible and stageable, make a dramatically compelling object of worship for those who put their trust in oratory rather than in Zeus: "they are the heavenly Clouds, magnificent goddesses for men / of leisure. They grace us with our intellect, argumentative skills, perception, / hyperbolization, circumlocution, pulverization, and predomination!" (316–318). Moreover, air and clouds have elaborate conventional metaphorical associations with intellectuals. The latter have their heads in the clouds (331–334); they are up in the air, as Socrates is when we first encounter him (219–234), rather than down to earth; and so on. Consequently, they offer Aristophanes a rich comic vein to mine.

We have good reason to think, then, that the majority of the specific scientific views attributed to Socrates in the play are not a product of Aristophanes' knowledge of Socrates himself, but a dramatic invention largely dictated by his primary role as a teacher of sophistic argument.

What, then, of sophistic argument? The problem here is that Aristophanes doesn't attribute any credible strategies of sophistic argument to Socrates. He claims, to be sure, that students can learn such argument from him (1147–1150). But what exactly they learn in learning it is left in the comic dark of jokes about the gender of nouns (658–694).

Though *Clouds* is lacking in the sort of detail on these matters that would lend it credibility as historical evidence, there is a general reason to believe that the portrait it presents of Socrates cannot be wholly wide of the mark. To achieve its comic purpose, *Clouds*, like all successful satire, had to be based on *something*. If the Socrates it presented was sufficiently unlike the Socrates the audience knew, it would fail.

The problem with this argument is that the basis successful satire needs is not fact, since the audience may be ignorant of that, but the audience's—possibly false—beliefs and prejudices. In the *Apology*, Socrates tells us what these were. His young followers imitate his elenctic techniques on others, who, as a result, charge him with corrupting the young. Moreover, certain charges were available in Athens against all philosophers, among them the charge of teaching atheistic scientific doctrines and sophist argument (23d2–9). The fact that *Clouds* may have been successful satire, then, does not entail that its portrait of Socrates be accurate.

Nonetheless, we are bound to feel as we read *Clouds* that Aristophanes is on to something about Socrates. But what exactly? Socrates characterizes Aristophanes as not attacking him, but a generic intellectual or sophist of his own invention. There is some suggestion in *Clouds*, however, that Aristophanes may have understood enough about elenctic philosophizing to have aimed some of his major criticisms at the narrower target. The competition between Superior and Inferior Argument, for example, which is the centerpiece of the play, looks something like an elenctic examination of the former by the latter. Inferior Argument uses things conceded by his opponent in order to refute him (942–943, 1037, 1314, 1040) and puts forward few substantive views of his own. True, Socrates is not presented as being Inferior's partisan—or Superior's either for that matter. But it is fair to say that he is shown as being in favor of something like elenctic discussion itself. It is up to Strepsiades to decide which argument his son will learn (937–938, 1105–1106). Socrates does not tell him which one to choose. Nonetheless, it is by watching the competition between them and seeing who comes out ahead that Socrates expects Strepsiades to reach his decision. The implication is that—whether it is Socrates' aim to teach it to them for this purpose or not—young people learn a skill from watching elenctic arguments, which, like Inferior Argument, enables them to argue down justice. And this, the play insists, results in their becoming moral and religious skeptics and corrupt opportunists.

Aristophanes may not have understood Socrates terribly well and may not have liked him. That weakens his testimony, such as it is, about the effects of the elenchus. But another witness—Plato—is unimpeachable on both counts. Yet his condemnation of the elenchus is, if anything, even stronger than Aristophanes': "We hold from childhood certain convictions about just and noble things; we're brought up with them as with our parents, we obey and honor them. . . . There are other ways of living, however, opposite to these and full of pleasures, that flatter the soul and attract it to themselves, but which don't persuade sensible people, who continue to honor and obey the convictions of their fathers. . . . And then a questioner comes along and asks someone of this sort, 'What is the noble?' And, when he answers what he has heard from the traditional lawgiver, the argument refutes him, and by refuting him often and in many places shakes him from his convictions and makes him believe that the noble is no more noble than shameful,[2] and the same with the just, the good, and the things he honored most. . . . Then when he no longer honors and obeys those convictions, and can't discover the true ones, will he be likely to adopt any other way of life than that which flatters him? . . . And so, I suppose, from being law abiding he becomes lawless" (*Republic* 538c–539a).

Neither of these attacks on the elenchus is decisive, of course, since each relies on controversial claims about its effects. But, decisive or not, they raise deep questions about Socrates and about the success of his service to Apollo—questions that have troubled Socrates' friends and foes ever since, and which we as readers must confront ourselves.

---

2. Compare *Clouds* 1019–1021: "He will have you believe that what should be shameful is beautiful [noble], and what should be beautiful [noble] is made shameful!"

Cast of Characters: *Clouds*

STREPSIADES   a rural Athenian

PHEIDIPPIDES   son of Strepsiades

HOUSEBOY   of Strepsiades

STUDENTS   of Socrates

SOCRATES   a philosopher

CHORUS   of Clouds

SUPERIOR ARGUMENT

INFERIOR ARGUMENT

FIRST CREDITOR

SECOND CREDITOR

CHAEREPHON   a philosopher

XANTHIAS   servant to Strepsiades

Clouds was first produced by Aristophanes in 423 B.C.E., at the Dionysia Festival in the city of Athens. This translation was inspired by a production by the London Small Theatre Company, which received its first U.K. public performance at the Shaw Theatre, London, in January 1990 and its first U.S. public performance at the Judith Anderson Theatre, New York, in May 1990, directed by Fiona Laird and produced by Peter Meineck.

Peter Meineck's *Clouds* first appeared in his *Aristophanes 1: Clouds, Wasps, Birds* (Indianapolis: Hackett Publishing Company, 1998). Some minor revisions in the translation have been made for its adaptation in the present volume.

CLOUDS

SCENE: *A house in Athens, which for more than seven years has been at war with Sparta. (An old man named Strepsiades and his son, Pheidippides, are asleep.*[1] *Strepsiades is tossing and turning and muttering to himself until he finally wakes up with a start.)*

STREPSIADES:
Oh! Oh!
Oh, Zeus almighty! What a night!
It's never ending! It must be morning soon.
I thought I heard the cock crow hours ago.
Just listen to those blasted servants, snoring away.   5
Back in my day they'd have never dared to sleep in.
Damn this stupid war! It'll ruin us. I can't even beat my own slaves anymore
in case they sneak off and hide out in enemy territory!

   (Pointing to Pheidippides.)

Just look at him, the "refined young gentleman." He'll never see the sunrise.
He'll just carry on, blissfully farting away under his five fluffy blankets.   10
It's all right for some! Oh, I'll just try and bury my head and ignore the snoring.

   (Strepsiades tries to go back to sleep. He tosses and turns and then angrily throws off the covers in frustration.)

It's no good, I just can't sleep!
I'm being bitten by debts and eaten away by stable bills.
Why? Because of this long-haired son of mine
and all his riding events and chariot races.   15
He lives, breathes, and dreams horses!
It's already the twentieth day of the month,
and the interest is due on the thirtieth. I'm finished!

---

1. The name means "son of Twister" and becomes appropriate through the course of the play as Strepsiades attempts to "twist" his way out of his debts. Pheidippides means something like "spare the horses."

89

(He calls out to a slave.)

Boy! Light a lamp and fetch my ledger!
20   I need to count up my debts and calculate the interest.

> *(A slave hurries onstage with some tablets and a lamp. He hands the
> tablets to Strepsiades and holds the lamp so he can read the accounts.)*

Now then, let's have a look at these debts:
"Twelve hundred drachmas owed to Pasias." Twelve hundred
    drachmas!
What on earth was that for? Oh, gods, I remember now, a horse
    for Pheidippides!
Twelve hundred drachmas? Ouch! I think I was the one taken for a
    ride.

PHEIDIPPIDES:
25   Philon, you cheat, keep to your own lane!

STREPSIADES:
You hear that! That's the problem right there.
He's constantly at the races, even in his sleep!

PHEIDIPPIDES:
How many turns must the war chariots make?

STREPSIADES:
Enough to turn your father into a pauper!
30   "What terrible debt shall strike after Pasias' bills?
Three hundred drachmas owed to Amynias
for a running board and a new set of wheels!"

PHEIDIPPIDES:
Make sure my horse has a roll before he goes home!

STREPSIADES:
It's my money those damned horses are rolling in!
While I am saddled with lawsuits and debts
35   and my creditors can't wait to seize my property.

(Pheidippides wakes up.)

PHEIDIPPIDES:
What is it, Father? Is it really necessary to spend
the entire night twisting and writhing about?

STREPSIADES:
   I'm being bitten to death . . . by bed bailiffs!

   (Pheidippides settles down back to sleep.)

STREPSIADES:
   Go on then, sleep away, soon enough all this will be yours.   40
   My debts will be on your head one day! Sleep away, my boy.
   Oh, I wish I had never met your mother, and I hope whoever it
      was
   who introduced us dies a horribly cruel death!
   Ah yes, those were the days, a lovely country life,
   full of simple rustic pleasures. An unwashed, unshaven heaven,
   abounding with honeybees, shaggy sheep, lashings of olive
      oil . . .   45
   then I married the niece of Megacles, son of Megacles.
   I was just a plain country boy, but she was from the city
   and had all these refined and delicate ways. A proper little lady.
   And when we were joined together as man and wife, I went to
      bed
   smelling fresh and fruity, like ripe figs and new wool.   50
   She smelled of fine perfume, golden saffron, sexy kisses,
   extravagance and luxury. Aphrodite all over and everywhere Eros.[2]
   Mind you, I can't say that she's lazy, not at all. She knew how to
      weave,
   if you know what I mean. In out, in out, she loved to poke the
      thread!
   It got to the point that I had to hold up my gown, show the
      evidence,
   and tell her that it would wear out if she kept on whacking it like
      that!   55

   (Strepsiades lifts his gown to reveal a limp phallus.)

HOUSEBOY:
   There's no oil left in the lamp.

STREPSIADES:
   Why did you use the thirstiest lamp in the house?
   You've earned a beating. Come here.

---

2. Aphrodite was the goddess of love, and Eros the god of love.

HOUSEBOY:
Why should I?

STREPSIADES:
Because you inserted a thick wick, that's why!

(The houseboy exits.)

60 Where was I? Oh yes. Well, soon enough we had a son,
and then my troubles really began. The wife and I could not agree
on a name for the boy. She wanted something upper class and
    horsey;
a name with *hippus* in it,[3] like "Xanthippus," "Chaerippus," or
    "Callippides."
But I wanted to name him Pheidonides[4] after his grandfather,
a good old-fashioned thrifty name.
65 We argued for ages; then eventually we reached a compromise
and gave him the name Pheidippides.
When he was little she used to take him in her arms and say,
"When you grow up, you'll be a rich man like Uncle Megacles[5]
and drive a chariot through the city wearing a beautiful golden
70   robe."[6]
But I would tell him, "When you're big you'll be just like your
    father
and drive goats down from the mountains, wearing a lovely leather
    jerkin."
But he never listened to a single word I said,
it was like flogging a dead horse, and now the household accounts
75 have a severe case of "galloping consumption."
I've been up all night trying to concoct a plan to get me out of this
    mess,
and I have found one drastic course, an extraordinary, supernatural
    trail.
If I can only persuade the lad to take it, I'll be saved!

---

3. Names containing *hippus* ("horse") were popular with the Athenian upper classes. Aristophanes' own father was named Phillippus.

4. Pheidonides means "son of Thrifty."

5. Megacles was a common name in the prominent aristocratic Alcmaeonid clan.

6. A victory in the Panathenaic games won the charioteer the right of riding in the procession to the Acropolis wearing a golden cloak.

Now then, let me think what would be the gentlest way to wake
  him up . . . ?

(Strepsiades leans over and whispers in Pheidippides' ear.)

Pheidipoo, little Pheidipoo . . .   80

*(There is no response from Pheidippides. Strepsiades becomes
frustrated and shouts.)*

PHEIDIPPIDES!

(Pheidippides wakes with a start.)

PHEIDIPPIDES:
  What! What do you want, Father?

STREPSIADES:
  Give me a kiss and take my hand.

(He does so.)

PHEIDIPPIDES:
  All right. What is it?

STREPSIADES:
  Tell me, son, do you love me?

PHEIDIPPIDES:
  By Poseidon,[7] god of horses, of course I do!

STREPSIADES:
  I don't want to hear about the god of horses!
  He's the very reason that I'm in this mess.   85
  Listen, son, if you really love me, will you do what I ask?

PHEIDIPPIDES:
  What would you like me to do?

STREPSIADES:
  Turn your life around, right now.
  Do what I say, and go and learn.

---

7. Poseidon was the second patron deity of Athens after Athena. He was god of
the sea, "Earthshaker," and father of horses.

PHEIDIPPIDES:
90   Learn what?

STREPSIADES:
Will you do it?

PHEIDIPPIDES:
(Exasperated.) I'll do it, by Dionysus![8]

STREPSIADES:
Great! Now look over there.
Can you see that tiny doorway and that funny little house?

PHEIDIPPIDES:
I see it. What are you showing me, Father?

STREPSIADES:
95   That, my boy, is the house of clever souls, the Pondertorium.
The men who live there are able to talk us into believing
that the universe is a casserole dish that covers us all
and we are the hot coals, nestling inside.
What's more, for a small fee, these gentleman will teach you
how to successfully argue any case, right or wrong.

PHEIDIPPIDES:
100   Who are these people?

STREPSIADES:
I'm not sure I know their names, but they are all gentlemen,
good and true, and fine philosophers of the finite.

PHEIDIPPIDES:
Ughh! I know who you mean, that godforsaken bunch
Of pasty-looking frauds, going around barefoot!
You're talking about Socrates and Chaerephon![9]

STREPSIADES:
105   Shut up! Stop talking like a baby.
Consider your father's daily bread. There'll be none left,
unless you give up horse racing and sign up for classes.

---

8. Dionysus was the god of wine, revelry, and the theater.
9. See Plato, *Apology* 20e8 note.

PHEIDIPPIDES:

No, by Dionysus, no! Not even if you gave me
a pair of Leogoras' finest pheasants![10]

STREPSIADES:

Please! My darling little boy, I beg you. Go and be taught.   110

PHEIDIPPIDES:

But what do I need to learn?

STREPSIADES:

I have heard it said, that in this house reside two different
kinds of argument, one is called the Superior Argument,
whatever that is, and the other is known as the Inferior Argument.
Some men say that the Inferior Argument can debate an unjust
    case   115
and win. All you have to do is learn this Inferior Argument for me.
Then you can talk your way out of all the debts I've incurred
on your behalf, and I won't have to repay a single obol.[11]

PHEIDIPPIDES:

No, I won't do it! How could I bear to show my pallid face
to all my friends in the cavalry?[12] Wild horses couldn't drag me in
    there!   120

STREPSIADES:

Then get out of my house, by Demeter![13] You'll not get another
crumb out of me. And that goes for your chariot stallion and your
    branded
thoroughbred. I've had enough of your horsing around!

PHEIDIPPIDES:

I'll just go to Uncle Megacles. He'll make sure   125
that I'm not without horse and home!

---

10. Aristocratic young men often kept birds. Pheasants were a rare species in
Greece and an expensive luxury.

11. An obol was a small Athenian coin. Six obols were equal to one drachma.

12. The Athenian cavalry (*hippeis*) was an exclusive corps of around a thousand
wealthy young upper-class citizens who could afford the expense of a horse and
armor.

13. Demeter was the goddess of the harvest.

(Exit Pheidippides.)

STREPSIADES:
I'm not down and out yet! With the help of the gods,
I'll enroll at the Pondertorium and learn it all myself!

(Strepsiades strides off, then slows down and stops.)

Oh, I'm just a stupid old fool. How on earth can I be expected
to learn all those hair-splitting arguments at my age?
130   I'm far too old, and my mind's certainly not what it used to be.

*(He turns around and sets off in the opposite direction, then sud-
denly stops.)*

No! I have to do it! It's my one and only chance.
No more delaying. I'm going to walk right up and knock on the
door!

*(He marches purposefully up to the door, knocks hard, and
shouts out.)*

Boy! Boy! Where are you? Boy!

(The stage left door hatch opens suddenly.)

STUDENT:
Go to hell!

*(The student slams the hatch shut. Strepsiades knocks on the door
again, and the hatch reopens.)*

Who's there?

STREPSIADES:
Strepsiades, son of Pheidon, from Cicynna.[14]

STUDENT:
Obviously an uneducated idiot! Don't you realize that you
135   thoughtlessly
banged away at the door with such force that you may well have
caused
the miscarriage of a brilliant new idea on the verge of discovery?

---

14. The exact location of Cicynna is not known, but it was probably a rural Attic
deme. See *Euthyphro* 2b9 note.

STREPSIADES:

I'm very sorry. I'm from far away, in the country.
What was it that may have "miscarried"?

(The student furtively looks around, then leans in to whisper.)

STUDENT:

Only students may be told such things. It is the sacred law.[15]   140

(Strepsiades mimics the student's movements and also whispers.)

STREPSIADES:

It's quite all right, you can tell me,
I've come to sign up as a student at the Pondertorium.

(The door opens, and the student breaks into normal speech.)

STUDENT:

Very well, but remember these things are holy mysteries and must
be kept secret. Just now, Socrates asked Chaerephon how many
feet a flea could jump, calculating the equation of one flea foot for
    a foot.   145
This question came to Chaerephon's mind, as the flea in question
had just bitten his eyebrow and leapt onto Socrates' head.

STREPSIADES:

How did he measure the distance?

STUDENT:

Expertly. He dipped the flea's feet in some melted wax,
and when it had dried, he carefully removed the molds,   150
producing a pair of Persian booties in miniature.
He was halfway through measuring the distance when you . . .

STREPSIADES:

Zeus almighty! What a delicate, subtle intellect!

STUDENT:

You should have heard the new concept that Socrates recently
    announced.

STREPSIADES:

What concept? Tell me, I beg you!   155

---

15. Compare *Apology* 33b6–9.

STUDENT:

Chaerephon of Sphettus[16] asked Socrates to pronounce
his opinion on an important scientific matter.

STREPSIADES:

What was that?

STUDENT:

Whether the hum of a gnat is generated via its mouth or its anus.

STREPSIADES:

Really? And what did he find out about the gnat?

STUDENT:

160   He said that the intestine of a gnat is extremely constricted
and that air is pressed through this narrow conduit to the anus.
Then the sphincter, acting as an oscillating cavity in close
    proximity
to a compressed channel, is forced to issue a vibrating sound
as a direct result of the wind acting upon it.

STREPSIADES:

165   So a gnat's ass is a trumpet! Who'd have thought it?
What an amazing display of rectumology; really gutsy stuff!
I'm sure Socrates could easily fend off
hostile legal actions with such a deep understanding of assholes.

STUDENT:

Yesterday he was robbed of a stupendous new idea by a speckled
    gecko.

STREPSIADES:

170   What? Tell me more.

STUDENT:

He was preoccupied studying the lunar revolutions,
and as he stood there gaping at the night sky,
a speckled gecko on the roof shat right on his head.

STREPSIADES:

(Laughing.) A speckled gecko shitting on Socrates! I like that.

---

16. An Attic deme. See *Euthyphro* 2b9 note.

STUDENT:

Then, last evening there was nothing for supper.   175

STREPSIADES:

Really? So how did he think he was going to get some oats?

STUDENT:

First, he laid the table by sprinkling a thin layer of ash over it,
then he bowed a skewer to form a pair of compasses, picked up
the bent legs . . . from the wrestling school and stole his cloak![17]

STREPSIADES:

Amazing! And to think, some people still think highly of Thales![18]   180
Come on, open, open the Pondertorium!
Quickly, I want to see him. I want to meet Socrates!
I can't wait any longer, I'm dying to learn. Open the door!

> *(The door opens. A group of four pallid, barefooted, and shabbily
> dressed students are revealed busy with various activities.)*

By Heracles! What on earth are these creatures?

STUDENT:

You seem surprised. What do you think they are?   185

STREPSIADES:

They look like a bunch of half-starved walking wounded to me.

> *(Pointing to a group of the students.)*

Why are they staring at the ground?

STUDENT:

They are seeking to know what lies beneath the earth.[19]

STREPSIADES:

I see. They're looking for onions to eat. They don't need to waste
time

---

17. This joke hinges on the word *diabētēs*, which can mean either a pair of compasses or "bestrider." The wrestling schools were popular places for meeting young men, and Socrates often spent time there.

18. Thales of Miletus (c. 625–c. 545 B.C.E.) was regarded as the father of natural philosophy.

19. Compare *Apology* 18b6–c1.

pondering about that. I know just where they can find some lovely
  big ones.
190   *(Pointing to another group.)* Why are they bending over like that?

STUDENT:

  They are probing the nether regions of Erebus deep beneath
    Tartarus.[20]

STREPSIADES:

  Really? So why are their asses pointing at the sky?

STUDENT:

  They are simultaneously studying "ass–stronomy!"
195   *(To the students.)* Back inside! He must not find you out here.

STREPSIADES:

  Hold on! Not so fast. Let them stay awhile,
  I'd like to probe them with a penetrating point.

STUDENT:

  Sorry. It's against all the rules. It's not good for them
  to spend too much time outside, exposed to the fresh air.

    *(Strepsiades notices a strange array of ludicrous scientific
    instruments.)*

STREPSIADES:

200   What, in the name of the gods, might these be?

STUDENT:

  This is for astronomy.

STREPSIADES:

  What's this for?

STUDENT:

  Geometry.

STREPSIADES:

  Geometry? What's that?

STUDENT:

  It is the science of measuring the land.

---

20. Erebus and Tartarus were the darkest and bleakest regions of Hades (the
Underworld).

STREPSIADES:
I see, to measure out plots for the landlords?

STUDENT:
No, to measure land generally.

STREPSIADES:
Lovely! What a very democratic mechanism. 205

(The student shows Strepsiades a large map.)

STUDENT:
This is a map of the entire world. Look, here is Athens.

STREPSIADES:
Don't be stupid, that can't be Athens!
Where are all the jurors and the law courts?

STUDENT:
I'm telling you, this area is clearly the region of Attica.

STREPSIADES:
So where's my deme then? Where's Cicynna? 210

STUDENT:
I don't know! Over there somewhere. You see here, that is Euboea,
the long island lying off the coast.

STREPSIADES:
Yeah, me and Pericles really laid those revolting bastards out![21]
Where's Sparta then?

STUDENT:
Right here.

STREPSIADES:
That's far too close! You need to move it immediately! 215
You had better re-ponder that one, mate!

STUDENT:
But it's simply not possible just to . . .

STREPSIADES:
Then you'll get a beating, by Zeus . . .

---

21. Euboea rebelled against Athenian control in 446 B.C.E. It was reconquered by
the Athenian democratic leader Pericles, who divided up much of the land and
awarded it to Athenian citizens.

(Enter Socrates suspended over the stage on a rack by the stage crane.)[22]

STUDENT:
Himself.

STREPSIADES:
Who's "Himself"?

STUDENT:
Socrates.

STREPSIADES:
220   Socrates! Call him over for me, will you?

STUDENT:
You call him! I'm, eh . . . very busy.

(Exit the student scurrying off.)

STREPSIADES:
Socrates! Oh Socrates!

SOCRATES:
Why do you call me, ephemeral creature?

STREPSIADES:
Socrates! What are you doing up there?

SOCRATES:
225   I walk the air in order to look down on the sun.

STREPSIADES:
But why do you need to float on a rack to scorn the gods?
If you have to do it, why not do it on the ground?

SOCRATES:
In order that I may make exact discoveries of the highest nature!
Thus my mind is suspended to create only elevated notions.
230   The grains of these thoughts then merge with the similar
atmosphere of thin air! If I had remained earthbound
and attempted to scrutinize the heights, I would have found
nothing; for the earth forces the creative juices to be drawn

---

22. See *Apology* 19c2–5.

to its core, depriving one of the all-important "water on the
brain!"[23]

STREPSIADES:

Eh?   235
You mean, you need a good brainwashing to think such thoughts?
Oh my dear Socrates, you must come down at once.
You must teach me all the things that I have come to learn.

(Socrates is lowered to the ground.)

SOCRATES:

And just why have you come?

STREPSIADES:

I want to learn to debate.
I'm being besieged by creditors, all my worldly goods   240
are under threat of seizure, the bailiffs are banging on my door!

SOCRATES:

Did you fail to realize you were amassing such enormous debts?

STREPSIADES:

Oh, I tried to keep things on a tight rein, but it was like closing
the stable door after the horse had bolted. I want you to teach me
that other Argument of yours, the one that never pays its dues.
Name your price, whatever it takes, I swear by the gods to pay
you!   245

SOCRATES:

(Laughing.) "Swear by the gods"? We don't give credit to the gods
here.

STREPSIADES:

Then how do you make oaths? Do you use those iron bars from
Byzantium?[24]

---

23. A parody of one of the main theories of the philosopher Diogenes of Apollonia, who believed that intellectual ability was influenced by moisture in the air. The dryer the air, the purer the thoughts. Because the earth held moisture, the nearer the ground a creature lived, the less intelligent it would be.

24. Byzantium was a Greek colony on the site of modern-day Istanbul. It used large heavy iron bars as currency, which were also thrown into the sea to seal oaths. The Spartans also used such currency, apparently to discourage the accumulation of wealth.

SOCRATES:
250   Do you really want to know the truth regarding matters divine?

STREPSIADES:
I do, by Zeus! Is that possible?

SOCRATES:
And do you wish communion with the Clouds, to actually speak
to our divinities?

STREPSIADES:
Oh yes, please!

SOCRATES:
Then lie down on this sacred couch.

STREPSIADES:
255   I'm lying down.

SOCRATES:
Here, take this ritual wreath.

STREPSIADES:
A wreath? Gods no! Socrates, I don't want to be sacrificed!
You're not going to make an Athamas out of me![25]

SOCRATES:
Don't worry, it's just a part of the initiation rites. Everyone has to
do it.

STREPSIADES:
What do I get out of it?

SOCRATES:
Why, you will become a polished public speaker, a rattling
260   castanet,
the "flour" of finest orators. Now hold still . . .

(Socrates sprinkles flour over Strepsiades.)

---

25. Athamas, a legendary Boeotian king, married Nephele ("Cloud") and had two
children by her, Phrixus and Helle. Ino, whom he married next, devised a false
prophecy that demanded the sacrifice of Nephele's children to curb a famine. But
Nephele saved them by flying them off on a golden ram. Athamas was then offered
for sacrifice in their place. Sacrificial victims were subsequently eaten.

STREPSIADES:

By Zeus, I'm no powder puff! I know when I'm getting a good
dusting!

SOCRATES:

Silence! Speak no ill words, old man, and heed my invocation.
O master, our lord, infinite Air, upholder of the buoyant earth.[26]
O radiant Ether, O reverend thunder-cracking Clouds, ascend!   265
Reveal yourselves, sacred ladies, emerge for those with higher
thoughts!

STREPSIADES:

Wait, wait! I need to wrap myself up first so I don't get soaked.
Dammit! I knew I shouldn't have left home without a hat.

SOCRATES:

Come, you illustrious Clouds, come and reveal yourselves to this
mortal.
From the sacred snow-capped crests of Olympus, from the festive
spiraling   270
dances of the Sea Nymphs in the lush gardens of the Ocean
father;
from the shimmering waters of the Nile where you dip your
golden goblets;
from Lake Maeotis or the icy heights of Mount Mimas.[27] Hear my
prayer!
Receive our sacrifice and bless our sacred rites.

(The Clouds are heard offstage.)

CHORUS:

Arise, appear, ever-soaring Clouds,
The shape of shimmering drops assume.   275
From mountain slopes where forests crowd,
From ocean depths where breakers boom.   280

---

26. The philosopher Diogenes (also parodied at 229–234) believed that the earth
was kept in position by air.

27. Lake Maeotis was the Greek name for the Sea of Azov to the north of the
Black Sea in the Crimea. Mount Mimas was the name of a mountain on the west
coast of modern-day Turkey opposite the island of Chios.

Look down upon the vales and hills,
See sacred earth where showers splash.
The holy rivers where rainfall spills,
285   The roaring sea's rush and dash.

Shake off the rain and misty haze,
A shining radiance warms the sky.
Upon this earth the Clouds will gaze
290   Under the tireless gleam of heaven's eye.

SOCRATES:
O magnificent, revered Clouds, you heard my summons. You
came!
Did you hear that sound? Those bellowing godlike thunderclaps?

STREPSIADES:
I revere you too, O illustrious Clouds! Let me answer your
rumbling part
with a rumbling fart! You've put the wind up me all right, I'm all a
jitter!
I don't know if it's right or wrong, but I need to take a thundering
295   crap!

SOCRATES:
Will you stop messing about and behaving like one of those
wretched comic playwrights!
Speak no ill words, a mighty flurry of goddesses is on the move,
singing as they go.

(The chorus begins to enter. Strepsiades still cannot see them.)

CHORUS:
300   On to Athens, maidens bearing rain,
The hallowed land of Cecrops' race,[28]
Mere the initiates seek to attain
Acceptance to a sacred place.

305   The house of Mysteries for holy rites[29]
And massive temples with statues grand.

---

28. Cecrops was the mythical original king of Athens, born from the earth of Attica.
29. The sanctuary at Eleusis, where religious initiation rites were held.

The godly processions to sacred sites,
The splendid sacrifices that crown the land.

Celebrations held throughout the year   310
Then sweet Dionysus comes in spring.
And the resonant tone of the pipes we hear
As the joyous chorus dance and sing.

STREPSIADES:

Zeus! Socrates, you must tell me, who are these ladies singing
this amazing song? Are they some new breed of female heroes?[30]   315

SOCRATES:

No, no, no. They are the heavenly Clouds, magnificent goddesses
    for men
of leisure. They grace us with our intellect, argumentative skills,
    perception,
hyperbolization, circumlocution, pulverization, and
    predomination!

STREPSIADES:

That's why my spirit has soared at the sound of their voices!
I'm raring to split hairs, quibble over windy intricacies, set notion   320
against notion, and strike down arguments within
    counterarguments!
Oh, Socrates, I can't wait any longer, I've just got to see them!

SOCRATES:

Then look over here, up at Mount Parnes.[31] Here they come,
delicately wafting down.

STREPSIADES:

Where? Where? I can't see! Show me.

SOCRATES:

There, there. Can you see them all? Floating down over hill and
    dale.
Look, there wafting toward us, to the left and right.   325

---

30. Heroes (often mythical) were cult figures, with a status somewhat like that of
Christian saints.

31. The highest peak in Attica, lying directly to the north of Athens.

STREPSIADES:
What on earth are you talking about? I can't see anything!

SOCRATES:
Look there, in the wings!

STREPSIADES:
Yes, I think I . . . I can just about make something out.

SOCRATES:
Are you completely blind? Surely you can see them now?

(The chorus is now assembled.)

STREPSIADES:
By Zeus! The illustrious ones themselves, they're everywhere, all around us!

SOCRATES:
And to think that you never knew they were goddesses. You had no faith.

STREPSIADES:
330   I thought they were just a load of old vapor, all drizzle and fog!

SOCRATES:
Exactly, because you were unaware that they cultivate a slew of sophisticated scholars;
prophets from the colonies, atmospheric therapists, long-haired loungers with jangling jewelry,
creators of complex, convoluted compositions, ethereal, immaterial, vacuous visionaries!
Intangible, insubstantial idleness sustained by waxing lyrical about the Clouds!

STREPSIADES:
Oh, I see! That's why they utter things like "the menacing storm
335   clouds advance, edged
with silver linings" and then call them "the billowing locks of hundred-headed Typhon,"[32]

---

32. Typhon was a mythological hundred-headed monster associated with violent storm winds.

"furious gusts," "sky-borne cisterns," "jagged clawed birds soaring
  through the air,"
and sing about "torrents pouring down from rain-filled clouds,"
  and for that load
of hot air they get rewarded with beautiful fillets of fish and lovely
  little roasted thrushes!

SOCRATES:
Just think, it's all due to the Clouds.   340

STREPSIADES:
But if they are supposed to be Clouds, why do they look like
  women?
What happened? The Clouds up in the sky don't look like
  that.

SOCRATES:
Well, what do they look like?

STREPSIADES:
I don't really know just how to describe them exactly. Like a flock
  of woolly sheepskin rugs;
certainly not like women. I've never seen a Cloud with a nose
  before.

SOCRATES:
Really? Then answer this one question.   345

STREPSIADES:
Ask away.

SOCRATES:
Have you ever looked up at the Clouds and thought that they
  seemed
to assume the shape of, say, a centaur, perhaps a leopard, or even a
  bull?

STREPSIADES:
I have, but so what?

SOCRATES:
The Clouds can assume any form they please. If they should
  happen to look down and spy

some long-haired, unkempt uncivilized type, say the son of
    Xenophantus,[33] for example,
then they assume the form of a centaur in recognition of his true
350   heart's desire.

STREPSIADES:

Ha! Then what if they see that fraudster, Simon,[34] who robbed the
    public funds?

SOCRATES:

Then they assume his true likeness and turn into wolves.

STREPSIADES:

Oh! Now I know why they looked like a herd of deer the other day.
They must have recognized Cleonymus,[35] the shield shedder, for
    the cowardly bastard that he is.

SOCRATES:

Precisely, and now they have obviously just seen Cleisthenes,[36]
355   hence they become women!

STREPSIADES:

O hail, divine ladies! Please do for me what you do for others,
sing a song to reach the very heights of heaven.

CHORUS:

(To Strepsiades.) Hail, O geriatric one, you who quest for artful words.
(To Socrates.) Hail priest of pedantic prattle, what would you bid
    us do?
360   There are only two ethereal experts we hearken to:
Prodicus,[37] for his sheer wisdom and knowledge, and you, for the
    way you strut around like a grand gander,

---

33. Identified as Hieronymus, a tragic playwright. His heart's desire was to have
the rampant sexual appetites and large penis of a Centaur—man above the waist,
horse below.

34. Probably a corrupt minor politician. Called a perjurer at 399 below.

35. Another minor Athenian politician, who was very fat.

36. Someone frequently ridiculed in Aristophanic comedy for his effeminate manner and lack of a beard.

37. Prodicus of Ceos was a sophist and contemporary of Socrates. He was chiefly
a teacher of rhetoric, with a special interest in the correct use of words and fine
distinctions of meaning.

roll your eyes, go barefoot, endure all, and hold such high
  opinions.

STREPSIADES:
  Good Earth! What vocals! Wondrous, sacred, marvelous!

SOCRATES:
  You see, these are the only true gods; everything else is utter
  nonsense.   365

STREPSIADES:
  What about Zeus? How can Olympian Zeus not be a god?

SOCRATES:
  Zeus? Don't be absurd! Zeus doesn't exist.

STREPSIADES:
  What are you saying? Who is it that makes rain, then?

SOCRATES:
  Why, the Clouds of course! I'll prove it to you. Does it ever rain
  without Clouds? No, and you would have thought that Zeus
    could   370
  have made rain on his own if he so desired, without the help of the
    Clouds.

STREPSIADES:
  And I always thought it was Zeus pissing through a sieve!
  You certainly have a way with words that makes complete sense.
  But hold on, who makes the thunder that makes me shake in
    terror?

SOCRATES:
  It is just the Clouds rocking in the sky.   375

STREPSIADES:
  Is nothing sacred! How do they do that?

SOCRATES:
  Simple. When they become completely saturated with moisture,
    they are forced
  by necessity to begin to oscillate to and fro. Every now and again
    they ram each other
  and of course, being packed with precipitation, CRASH! A
    cloudburst!

STREPSIADES:

But surely someone must force them to move in the first place.
That must be Zeus.

SOCRATES:

380   Not at all, it is the whirling of the Celestial Basin!

STREPSIADES:

Basin? So Zeus is no more and Basin is king now, is he?
But you haven't explained who it is that makes the thunder.

SOCRATES:

Listen! The Clouds become full of water and crash into each other,
thus they emit a thundering sound because of their sheer density.

STREPSIADES:

385   Do you seriously expect me to believe that?

SOCRATES:

Then allow me to demonstrate, using you as my example. Have
you ever been
at the Panathenaea festival[38] and eaten too much soup? What
happened?
Your stomach suddenly became upset and started to rumble, yes?

STREPSIADES:

Yes, by Apollo. It grumbles and groans with all that soup sloshing
around,
and then it makes a noise that sounds just like thunder. First of all
it's just a little splutter . . . Phuurrrt! Then it gets a bit louder. . .
390   PHHUuuuurrtt!
And when I finally get to take a shit, it really thunders just like
those clouds . . .
. . . PHHHAAAARRRAAATTT!

SOCRATES:

My dear old fellow, if a tiny stomach such as yours can emit such a
fart,
just think what a colossal thunder the vast atmosphere can
produce.

---

38. See *Euthyphro* 6c2 note.

STREPSIADES:

Yes, thunder and farter,[39] they even sound the same.

But what about those flashing, fiery shafts of lightning that can burn

us to a crisp or at the least give us a good grilling every now and then?

Surely that is Zeus' instrument against oath breakers.

SOCRATES:

You blithering, prehistoric, pre-Cronian old fool!

If Zeus smites oath breakers, why has he not incinerated Simon,

Cleonymus, or Theorus?[40] They couldn't break more oaths if they tried!

Instead he strikes the temple at Cape Sunium[41] and turns his own oak trees to charcoal.[42]

Everyone knows that an oath as solid as oak can't be broken.

What was he thinking?

STREPSIADES:

I don't know, but it all sounds very convincing. So what's a thunderbolt then?

SOCRATES:

When an arid gust is blown up above and becomes trapped inside the Clouds,

it tends to inflate them rather like a bladder; the sheer volume of air causes

the Clouds to explode, and the compressed hot wind is forced out with such

terrific energy that in the process it bursts into spontaneous flame.

STREPSIADES:

The exact same thing happened to me once at the Diasia feast.[43]

I was cooking a nice big sausage for the family, and I completely

395

400

405

410

---

39. In Greek, *brontē* and *pordē*. Etymology was an area of interest for the sophists. Here reduced to cheap toilet humor by Strepsiades.

40. Another minor politician.

41. See *Euthyphro* 43d3 note.

42. The oak tree was sacred to Zeus.

43. In honor of Zeus Meilichios ("the kindly one").

forgot to prick it. Well, it swelled right up and suddenly BANG!
It blew up right in my face and showered me with hot blood
and fat!

CHORUS:
You come craving knowledge of the highest kind
415 *So the Greeks will call you Athens' mastermind.*
If you possess a brain fit for cogitation
And can suffer cold, stress, and deprivation.
If you can pace about and stand for hours
Not drink nor train by sheer willpower,
If you hold the clever soul in high regard,
420 *Battling by the tongue will not be hard.*

STREPSIADES:
My mind never rests, I'm as tough as old boots.
I've a mean, lean stomach, and I can live on roots.
Fear not, there's nothing that this body can't handle;
I'm ready to temper my spirit upon your anvil!

SOCRATES:
And do you repudiate all other gods, except those we venerate,
the holy trinity of Chaos, Clouds, and a confident tongue?

STREPSIADES:
I wouldn't even speak to a god if I met one, and you won't catch
425 me
sacrificing, pouring libations, or burning incense on any of their
altars.

CHORUS:
Then tell us, what is it you would like us to do for you? We will
not fail you,
not if you pay us due honor and respect and come in search of
knowledge.

STREPSIADES:
Reverend ladies! It's just a tiny little thing that I ask of you;
I wish to be the finest speaker in all of Greece, a hundred times
430 over!

CHORUS:
So be it. From this day henceforth no man shall ever pass

more motions in the public assembly than you . . .

STREPSIADES:

    No, no, no! I'm not interested in politics and carrying on in the
        assembly!

    I want to twist Justice around and escape the clutches of my
        creditors.

CHORUS:

    Then you will have your heart's desire, it is but a small thing you
        require.   435

    Just place yourself into the hands of our leading devotees.

STREPSIADES:

    I'll do it! I have to! I've got no choice, you see!

    The horses and my marriage will be the death of me!

    So here I am, take me now, I'm yours!
    Beat me, bruise me, it's in a very good cause.   440
    I'll starve, not bathe, shiver, shake, and freeze,
    Feel free to tan my hide as often as you please!

    I'll do anything to avoid the paying of my debts,
    And men will come to realize my newly won assets.
    I'll be dangerous, mad, and devil-may-care,
    A low-down dirty liar, driven to despair!

    A courthouse junkie blessed with the gift of gab,
    A barrack-room lawyer and a filthy, oily rag!
    A chiseler, a shyster, a bullshitter and cheat,   450
    A miscreant, a twister, and a master of deceit!

    Feed me on chop logic, I'll feast on your split hairs,
    And all those who meet me should take extra care.
    So now I've told you what it is I yearn to be,   455
    Serve me to your students and make mincemeat out of me!

CHORUS:

    I can't help but admire
    his sheer strength of character.
    Let me tell you this.   460
    If you learn your lessons well,

your very name will reach up
to resound in the heights of heaven.

STREPSIADES:
Then what lies in store for me?

CHORUS:
For the rest of your days you will be
465   the most blessed and envied of all men.

STREPSIADES:
Really?

CHORUS:
Of course!
Crowds will gather at your door
clamoring for any opportunity
470   to actually get to talk to you.
They'll all come in supplication,
seeking your sage advice.
You'll help them to decide vitally important
and extravagantly expensive issues,
475   issues suited to such an intellect as yours.
Now to enroll this old man in our educational program;
it is time to stimulate his mind and test his knowledge.

SOCRATES:
So, tell me a little about yourself.
I need to understand your particular personality traits.
480   Then I can correctly determine the best tactics to deploy.

STREPSIADES:
Tactics? Are you planning to lay siege to me?

SOCRATES:
No, no, I just want to analyze you a little.
Now then, are you in possession of a powerful memory?

STREPSIADES:
Well, that all depends. If someone owes me money,
485   it is quite superb, but if, on the other hand, I owe money,
then I'm afraid it has a tendency to let me down.

SOCRATES:
Then perhaps you have a particular penchant for oral recitation?

STREPSIADES:

(*Laughing.*) Me? I'm certainly reticent to pay my debts!

SOCRATES:

Look, how on earth do you expect to learn anything?

STREPSIADES:

Oh, don't be such a worrier. I'll get the hang of it.

SOCRATES:

All right then, make sure that whenever I throw out some juicy
  bits
of heavenly wisdom that you snatch them up right away.   490

STREPSIADES:

(*Laughing.*) What do you take me for, a dog?

SOCRATES:

You utter, uneducated barbarian oaf!
We may well have to beat some sense into this old fool.
Tell me, what would you do if someone were to hit you?

STREPSIADES:

I'd fall over! And I'd stay down too, at least until a witness   495
came along. Then I'd go and file assault charges
and get a hefty out-of-court settlement or some nice damages!

SOCRATES:

Remove your outer garment.

STREPSIADES:

What for, am I in trouble already?

SOCRATES:

No, all new initiates must disrobe.

STREPSIADES:

But I promise I won't steal anything inside.

SOCRATES:

Just take the damn thing off, will you!   500

> (*Strepsiades takes off his tunic and gives it to Socrates, leaving him
> naked except for a loincloth.*)

STREPSIADES:
> If I work really hard and attend to my studies,
> which of your followers can I ever hope to be like?

SOCRATES:
> You should try to be like Chaerephon.

STREPSIADES:
> Good gods no, I'll be as good as dead!

SOCRATES:
505   Will you please stop jabbering away.
> Get a move on and follow me!

STREPSIADES:
> All right, all right, but at least put a honey cake in my hand.
> I'm scared; it's like descending into Trophonius' grotto.[44]

SOCRATES:
> Stop dillydallying at the door and come on!

(Enter Socrates and Strepsiades into the Pondertorium.)

CHORUS:
510   *Good luck to this brave soul,*
> *Embarking on his quest,*
> *Though he's old and gray*
> *I know he'll do his best.*
> *A dyed-in-the-wool spirit*
515   *Dipping into new ideas,*
> *Such a radical education*
> *For a man of advanced years.*

[Parabasis]

(The chorus leader addresses the audience, speaking for Aristophanes.)

CHORUS:
> Dear audience, allow me to speak candidly for a moment.
> It is time to hear the truth, sworn by Dionysus, the very deity

---

44. The subterranean oracular shrine of the hero Trophonius in Boeotia contained sacred snakes, which initiates placated with honey cakes.

that nurtured my rare talent and raised me to win great dramatic
    victories.   520
I thought that you were an intelligent audience, I thought that you
    would
truly enjoy this, the most intellectual of all my comedies.
I sweated night and day over a hot script to serve up to you
the very first taste of the fruits of my labor. But look what
    happened.
I was utterly defeated, thwarted by those other vile, despicable
    hacks![45]   525
And it is you people who must bear the blame for this disgrace,
for you should have known better. I did it all for you, and just look
    how you chose
to repay me! But never fear, I will always be here for those with
    the good taste
to fully appreciate the quality of my work. It was here, in this very
    theater,
that my tale of the righteous boy and the little bugger was so very
    well received.[46]   530
It is true that I was not yet of an age to mother properly such a
    child, and so I exposed
my prodigy to be adopted by another in my stead. Then you, dear
    audience, you all
became its foster parents. It was you who nurtured it, you who
    raised it.
Ever since then I have held you all in the highest esteem, and I
    always swore by your sound judgment and prudent wisdom.
    And now like Electra,   535
this comedy comes searching, hoping, seeking an audience equal
    in wit and intelligence,
and like the hair on Orestes' head, she'll know them when she sees
    them![47]

---

45. The reference is to the original version of *Clouds*, performed in 423 B.C.E. It placed third and last behind Cratinus' *Wine Flask* (first) and Ameipsias' *Connus* (second). At some point Aristophanes began to revise the play, but he never completed the revision. The revised version is the only one we now possess.

46. Aristophanes' first play, *Banqueters* (427 B.C.E.), which placed second.

47. In Aeschylus' *The Libation Bearers* (164–200), Electra—the daughter of Agamemnon and Clytemnestra, his murderer—comes to the tomb of her father, and

Contemplate for a moment, if you will, the value of her discreet
    sensibilities.
She does not dangle one of those huge, red-tipped appendages
540   between her legs to get cheap laughs from the children among you.[48]
She doesn't make rude jibes at the expense of bald men, and she
    categorically refuses
to perform any kind of suggestive dances. You will never see her
    leading actor
dressed up as an old man, running around, hitting all and sundry
    with a stick
to divert your attention from the poor quality of the rotten old
    jokes! What's more
you will certainly not encounter anybody charging onstage with
    flaming torches,
shouting Oh! Oh! No, this play comes here today trusting only in
545   itself and its poetry,
and I, the playwright, am cast from the same mold. I have always
    been bold
(bold, not bald—I know I'm bald!), and I have never ever
    attempted to bamboozle you
by rehashing the same tired old material time and time again. No,
    I devote
every strain of my poetic fiber to the invention of brand-new,
    cutting-edge comedy.
Every play has something different, something innovative,
    vivacious, and skillful.
When Cleon[49] was at the peak of his powers, I slugged him in the
550   stomach,
but I never hit the man when he was down. But just look at my
    rivals and how they

---

there she recognizes a lock of the hair belonging to Orestes, signaling his return
from exile.

48. It is unclear whether Aristophanes is alluding to real children or to childish
adults. A large phallus was a frequent comic prop.

49. The son of a wealthy tanner and one of the first of a new breed of Athenian
politicians who were not from old aristocratic families and whose power depended
on their rhetorical skills in the courts and before the Assembly rather than on public office. A frequent butt of comedy, he attacked Aristophanes' *Babylonians* in 436
B.C.E. for slandering the state.

treated Hyperbolus.[50] They walked all over him, not to mention
   the punishment they dealt out to his poor old mother! It all
   started with Eupolis[51] and that dreadful farce
of his, *Maricas*, blatant plagiarism! A disgusting imitation of my
   Knights with the totally
unnecessary addition of an inebriated old hag crudely gyrating in
   the dances.   555
The very same character, might I add, that we saw Phrynichus[52]
   present
in his comedy about the women being fed to the sea creature!
Then came Hermippus,[53] and his vicious attacks on Hyperbolus.
Soon everyone jumped on the Hyperbolus bandwagon and were
   happily
dishing out the dirt, and worst of all stealing all my best eel gags!   560
If you find that kind of drivel amusing, you will never fully
   appreciate my work,
but those who enjoy my comedic innovations will be considered
   wise in years to come.

Zeus the highest god of all,
Greatest ruler, hear our call.

Come, Poseidon, with trident flashing,   565
From salty depths with breakers crashing.

The sky father that witnessed our birth
Most sacred nurturer of life on earth.

The charioteer who fills our days,
With the light, heat, and brilliant rays.[54]

---

50. A politician who became prominent after the death of Cleon in 422 B.C.E.

51. One of the most highly regarded Athenian comic playwrights. His work sur-
vives only in fragments. He produced his first play in 429 B.C.E. and won at least
seven victories. Hyperbolus' mother appears in his *Maricas*, produced in 421 B.C.E.

52. Another contemporary Athenian comic playwright.

53. Hermippus' play *Bread Sellers*, produced in 420/19 B.C.E., attacked Hyperbolus and his mother.

54. Helios, the sun god, who drives his chariot from the east to the west, bringing
daylight.

To god and mortal, great power advance,
We call you all to join our dance!

    (The Clouds address the audience.)

Attention please, audience! It is time to prick your collective
575   conscience.
You have performed us a great disservice, and we are here to
     chastise you for it!
No deity gives more to this city than we, and yet you fail to pay us
     the slightest respect!
We are the ones who are ever present, and we constantly have your
     best interests
at heart, but you never pour us any libations or even offer a single
     sacrifice!
When you are about to embark on some futile armed campaign,
580   we bellow noisily
and send sheets of rain. When you were holding elections for
     general and chose
that damned Paphlagonian tanner, we frowned down and
     thundered our dissent.
"Such sheets of fire, such bursts of horrid thunder." Even the
     moon reversed
her course, and the very sun in the sky snuffed his great wick and
585   announced
that he would not rekindle his heavenly light if you nominated
     Cleon as general![55]
But in spite of everything, you still went ahead and voted for the
     man!
It has been said that bad decisions run rife in this city, and yet
     somehow the gods
always conspire to make everything turn out for the best. It is the
     same in this instance,
for there is a simple solution to turn this terrible error of judgment
590   to your advantage.
Just go ahead and indict that gannet Cleon on charges of fraud and
     embezzlement,

---

55. Cleon ("that damned Paphlagonian tanner") was elected as one of Athens' ten
generals in March 424/3 B.C.E. There was a lunar eclipse on 29 October and a
solar eclipse on 21 March.

clap him in the stocks and lock him up. Lo and behold, out of
    your previous folly
shall come your salvation. Everything will be as before,
back the way things were, to the very great benefit of your city.

Come, Phoebus Apollo, lord of Delos,   595
Leave Cynthus' rocks and come to us.

Come, Artemis,[56] *leave your house of gold,*
Worshipped by Lydian daughters age old.

Goddess of the Aegis, protector of our city,   600
Lady Athena, held in highest sanctity.

From Parnassus' towering heights,
Setting ablaze his pine torch light,

The Bacchants of Delphi, wild and joyous,   605
Come, festive god, come, Dionysus.

LEADER:
    When we were on our way here, we happened to meet the Moon,
    Who told us to relay her benedictions to the Athenians and their
        allies.
    However, she also informed us that she is very cross with you   610
    and that you have treated her with disrespect, despite all
    the wonderful things she has done for you all. Just think, she saves
    you at least a drachma a month for all the torches you have no
        need of.
    She's heard you telling your houseboys, "Don't bother with the
        lamp tonight, my lad, the moonlight's nice and bright.   615
    She does that for you and a lot more besides! She also informed us
        that she is most displeased with all this fiddling about with the
        lunar cycle.[57]

---

56. Daughter of Zeus and Leto and twin sister of Apollo.
57. Each Greek city utilized its own dating system, though they were all based on
the lunar cycle. In Athens there were twelve months, each named after a festival.
The year started with the first new moon after the summer solstice, and each sub-
sequent month was marked by the falling of the old moon, indicating the end of

She says it is playing absolute havoc with the calendar, and she has
    received numerous
complaints from angry gods who have been cheated out of their
    due festival days!
To top it all, on sacred sacrificial days you are going around,
620   torturing people
and sitting in court passing judgment when you should be
    worshipping.
There have even been times when the gods were partaking in a
    solemn memorial
service to Memnon or Sarpedon[58] while you lot were pouring
    libations, drinking
and cavorting about all over the city—disgraceful! That is why
    Hyperbolus,
your elected religious remembrancer,[59] had his wreath removed by
625   the gods.
Now he knows that you should arrange your dates in concordance
    with the Moon!

    (Enter Socrates.)

SOCRATES:
By Breath, by Chaos, by Air!
I have never before encountered such a feeble-minded, imbecilic,
    slow-witted country bumpkin in all my life!
630 He forgets the tiniest scraps of knowledge
before he's even had a chance to learn them!

    (Calling into the Pondertorium.)

Strepsiades! Come on out here, into the light.

---

one month, and the rising of the new moon, indicating the beginning of another.
Therefore, Athenian months lasted twenty-nine or thirty days. The last day of the
month was called the "old-and-new day." It seems that Athenian officials could
adjust the calendar to suit particular civic needs such as the postponement or re-
scheduling of festivals, therefore causing the calendar to fall out of synchronization
with the moon.

58. Two heroes killed in the Trojan War.

59. Holders of this office represented Athens at the Amphictyonic council at Delphi, which was responsible for religious sanctuaries and the maintenance of their
cults.

Hurry up, and bring the couch with you.

(Enter Strepsiades, still seminaked, carrying a small couch. Like Socrates, he is now barefoot.)

STREPSIADES:
No need, the flea-infested thing can get up and walk out on its own!

SOCRATES:
Put it down over there and listen carefully.   635

STREPSIADES:
All right.

SOCRATES:
Good, let's get started. Which facet of your intellect do you wish to develop?
Perhaps you would like to use this opportunity to master a subject you never had
the opportunity to learn before? Meter? Rhythm? Scales?

STREPSIADES:
Scales! Only the other day that bastard grain merchant fiddled me out of a full two measures!   640

SOCRATES:
Not those kind of scales, you idiot! I'm attempting to engage you in a discussion
on music and poetry. Now, consider which measure is more aesthetically pleasing,
the three-quarter beat or the four-quarter beat?

STREPSIADES:
Personally, I think the pint takes some beating!

SOCRATES:
Will you stop babbling such utter nonsense!

STREPSIADES:
It's not nonsense. Everyone knows four quarts makes a pint!   645

SOCRATES:
Oh damn you! You illiterate uneducated peasant!
Let's at least see if you can learn something about rhythm.

STREPSIADES:
Rhythm? How is learning about rhythm going to buy me barley?

SOCRATES:
A detailed knowledge of rhythm enables you to socialize
     effectively in polite
company and seem refined and cultured. You'll know all about
650   martial modes
and dactylic meter . . .

(Strepsiades looks confused.)

beating the rhythm with your fingers!

STREPSIADES:
I know how to beat with my fingers, by Zeus!

SOCRATES:
You do? Tell me about it.

STREPSIADES:
Well, when I was a young lad it was this . . .

(Strepsiades grabs and strokes his phallus.)

SOCRATES:
655   Gods! You are nothing but a village idiot!

STREPSIADES:
You're the idiot. I don't want to learn any of this stuff.

SOCRATES:
Well, what DO you want to learn?

STREPSIADES:
The other thing, you know: *(Whispering.)* The Wrong Argument.

SOCRATES:
That's an advanced class. You can't just start there. You have to
     master the basics first, such as the correct gender affiliation of
     certain types of quadrupedic livestock.

STREPSIADES:
660   Livestock! I'm an expert. Let's see, masculine:
Ram, billy goat, bull, dog, chicken . . .

SOCRATES:
And the feminine?

STREPSIADES:
Ewe, nanny goat, cow, bitch, chicken[60] . . .

SOCRATES:
Aha! You called both the male and the female chicken.
You can't do that!

STREPSIADES:
What do you mean?

SOCRATES:
You said "chicken" and "chicken."

STREPSIADES:
By Poseidon, you're right! Well, what should I have said?   665

SOCRATES:
Chicken . . . and chickeness!

STREPSIADES:
Chickeness? That's a good one, by Air!
For just that single piece of learning
I should fill your meal kneader with barley oats.[61]

SOCRATES:
You've done it again, said another one. You used the masculine
    form   670
for meal kneader, but it really should be feminine.[62]

STREPSIADES:
What? I made a meal kneader masculine?

SOCRATES:
Yes, just like Cleonymus.

STREPSIADES:
What do you mean?

---

60. *Alektruōn* was used for both the cock and the hen.

61. *Cardopus* was a troughlike kneading tray with a large pestle that was used like a rolling pin. Barley was a cheap food but also part of many sacred festivals and initiation rites.

62. *Cardopus* is feminine, though it appears to have a masculine ending.

SOCRATES:
Meal kneader and Cleonymus are treated in the same manner.

STREPSIADES:
675   But Socrates, Cleonymus doesn't even own a meal kneader.
His "needs" are met by having his oats delivered by the back
    door,[63]
if you, eh, know what I mean! What should I call it from now on?

SOCRATES:
The feminine form, that is, "fe-meal kneader."

STREPSIADES:
So a meal kneader needs a female to be a fe-meal kneader?

SOCRATES:
Exactly.

STREPSIADES:
680   I see. So I should have said, Cleonymus never needed a female?

SOCRATES:
Yes. Well then, we must still educate you on proper names.
You need to know which are masculine and which are feminine.

STREPSIADES:
I know which are feminine all right.

SOCRATES:
Go on then.

> *(Strepsiades lustfully imagines a group of well-known Athenian
> beauties.)*

STREPSIADES:
Lysilla *(Wow whee!)*, Philinna *(Oh yeah!)*, Cleitagora *(Hubba,
hubba!)*, and Demetria *(Ow!)*.

SOCRATES:
685   And the masculine names?

> *(He imagines a collection of effeminate young men.)*

STREPSIADES:
There's plenty: Philoxenus *(Luvvie!)*, Melesias *(Big Boy!)*, Amynias
(Hello sailor!) . . .

---

63. That is, he adopts the female role by submitting to anal intercourse.

SOCRATES:
Those are hardly masculine!

STREPSIADES:
You don't think they're masculine?

SOCRATES:
Absolutely not. If you saw Amynias, just how would you call out
    to him?

STREPSIADES:
Like this: "Coo-ee! Coo-ee! Amynia luvvie! Amynia darling!"   690

SOCRATES:
I rest my case. You are clearly calling out to him like a woman,
and what's more, "Amynia" is feminine.

STREPSIADES:
That's what the old poof gets for dodging the draft.
But everyone knows Amynias is an old woman. I don't need to be
    taught that.

SOCRATES:
Be quiet, by Zeus! Now lie down on the couch there.

STREPSIADES:
What for?

SOCRATES:
You need to concentrate on personal matters.   695

STREPSIADES:
No, I'm begging you! Don't make me lie down there. I can just as
    easily
do my personal concentrating on the bare earth!

SOCRATES:
I'm sorry, you simply have no choice.

STREPSIADES:
Oh no! Those fleas are going to have a field day feasting on me!

    (Exit Socrates.)

CHORUS:
So philosophize and cogitate,   700
Intellectualize and ruminate.

Twist your thoughts, your mind must bend,
Through mental blocks and each dead end.
Let ideas jump and concepts fly,
705   *Don't let sweet sleep close your eyes.*

STREPSIADES:
Oh! Woe! Oh! Woe!

CHORUS:
What pains thee? Art thou smitten?

STREPSIADES:
Misery! Agony! I'm being bitten!
They're leaping off this bed and biting
710   *Like Corinthians fleeing from the fighting!*[64]
They've been gnawing on my bones all day,
They're sucking all my blood away!
They've champed my bollocks all red raw,
My poor old ass has never felt this sore!
715   *These bugs will chew me half to death . . .*

CHORUS:
I suggest you give that moaning a rest!

STREPSIADES:
Some help you are, what bad advice!
I've lost money and health for a load of lice!
My very soul is bruised and beaten,
720   *My clothes and shoes are all moth eaten.*
So I sing to keep my spirits high,
But it's all over now, the end is nigh!

(Enter Socrates.)

SOCRATES:
What are you doing? You are supposed to be contemplating.

STREPSIADES:
I am, by Poseidon.

SOCRATES:
And just what, pray, have you been contemplating?

---

64. "Corinthians" seems to have been an Athenian slang term for "bedbugs" or "fleas," derived from a simple pun on *koreis* (bugs) and *Korinthioi* (Corinthians).

STREPSIADES:
  I've been contemplating my future, once these bugs have finished
    me off!   725

SOCRATES:
  Go to hell!

STREPSIADES:
  Hell's right, chum! That's exactly what this is.

CHORUS:
  Don't be so fainthearted. Cover yourself up
  and devise some fraudulent and illicit affair.

STREPSIADES:
  Oh, if only instead of these lambskin covers,
  I could get into an illicit affair!   730

  *(Strepsiades covers himself up and lies on the couch. He wriggles
  about; and then the covers rise, propped up by his phallus. Socrates
  reenters.)*

SOCRATES:
  All right, let's see how he's doing.
  You there! Are you sleeping?

  (Strepsiades pops his head out from under the fleece.)

STREPSIADES:
  No, by Apollo, not me, no.

SOCRATES:
  Have you been able to get a good grasp on anything?

STREPSIADES:
  Eh . . . well, no, not really.

SOCRATES:
  Nothing whatsoever?

STREPSIADES:
  Well, my right hand has a good grasp on my prick at the moment.

  (Strepsiades removes the covers to reveal his erect phallus.)

SOCRATES:
  Oh, by all the gods! Cover yourself up at once and think about
    something else!   735

STREPSIADES:
But what? Tell me, Socrates, please.

SOCRATES:
No, you must discover that for yourself, then tell me what it is you
want.

STREPSIADES:
But you know very well what I want, I've told you a thousand
times:
It's my debts. I want to get out of paying them off!

SOCRATES:
740   All right then. Cover yourself up and dissect your suppositions
into microscopic elements. Then consider the matter in minute
detail
thus arriving at a correct analysis derived from an orthodox
methodology.

*(Strepsiades pulls the fleece over his head and fidgets for a while
before lying down.)*

STREPSIADES:
Ohh! Ahh!

SOCRATES:
Stop fidgeting! Now, should your concept place you in a quandary
move on, free your mind. Then the idea
can be set in motion once the innermost recesses of your intellect
745   have been unlocked.

(Strepsiades uncovers himself.)

STREPSIADES:
My beloved Socrates!

SOCRATES:
What is it?

(Strepsiades gets up on his feet and runs toward Socrates.)

STREPSIADES:
I've thought of an illicit idea for avoiding my debts!

SOCRATES:
Do divulge.

STREPSIADES:
  Tell me this . . .

SOCRATES:
  What, what?

STREPSIADES:
  What if I got hold of a witch from Thessaly[65]
  and made her magic the moon out of the sky?   750
  I could put it away in a dressing case like a mirror
  and hide it where no one would ever find it.

SOCRATES:
  But how would that help you?

STREPSIADES:
  How? If I stopped the moon from rising, then I would never have
    to pay the interest on any of my debts.   755

SOCRATES:
  Why ever not?

STREPSIADES:
  Because interest is always due at the end of the month, when the
    new moon appears!

SOCRATES:
  I see. Here's another situation to consider. What would you do
  if a lawsuit was written up against you for five talents[66] in damages?
  How would you go about having the case removed from the
    record?

STREPSIADES:
  Er, I've no idea, let me have a think about it.   760

  (Strepsiades goes back under the fleece.)

SOCRATES:
  Be sure not to constrict your imagination by keeping your
    thoughts wrapped up.
  Let your mind fly through the air, but not too much. Think of
    your creativity

---

65. The reputation of Thessalian women for sorcery was proverbial.
66. Thirty thousand drachmas.

as a beetle on a string, airborne, but connected, flying, but not too
   high.[67]

(He pops up from under the cover.)

STREPSIADES:
   I've got it! A brilliant way of removing
   the lawsuit! You're going to love this one.

SOCRATES:
765   Tell me more.

STREPSIADES:
   Have you seen those pretty see-through stones that the healers sell?
   You know, the ones they use to start fires.

SOCRATES:
   You mean glass.[68]

STREPSIADES:
   That's the stuff! If I had some glass, I could secretly position myself
      behind
   the bailiff as he writes up the case on his wax tablet. Then I could
770   aim the sun's rays
   at his docket and melt away the writing so there would be no
      record of my case!

SOCRATES:
   Sweet charity! How "ingenious."

STREPSIADES:
   Great! I've managed to erase a five-talent lawsuit.

SOCRATES:
   Come on, then, chew this one over.

STREPSIADES:
775   I'm ready.

SOCRATES:
   You're in court, defending a suit, and it looks like you will surely
      lose.

---

67. In a popular child's game, a beetle would be tied by a string to a stone or other
heavy object and forced to fly.

68. Glass was a rare and expensive commodity at this time.

It's your turn to present your defense, and you have absolutely no
   witnesses.
How would you effectively contest the case and, moreover, win
   the suit itself?

STREPSIADES:
Easy!

SOCRATES:
Let's hear it then.

STREPSIADES:
During the case for the prosecution,
I would run off home and hang myself!   780

SOCRATES:
What are you talking about?

STREPSIADES:
By all the gods, it's foolproof! How can anybody sue me when I'm
   dead?

SOCRATES:
This is preposterous! I've had just about enough of this!
You'll get no more instruction from me.

STREPSIADES:
But Socrates, in the name of heaven, why not?

SOCRATES:
Because if I do manage to get something through to you, it is
   instantly   785
forgotten. Here, I'll prove it. What was the first thing I taught you?

STREPSIADES:
Mmmm, the first lesson, hang on, let me think, what was that, uh,
something female where we scatter our oats, oh I don't know!

SOCRATES:
You fossilized, forgetful old fool! Just piss off!   790

   (Exit Socrates in disgust.)

STREPSIADES:
Oh no! I'm finished. This is terrible!
If I don't learn tongue twisting, then I'm lost without a hope!
Clouds! You have to help me out. What can I do?

CHORUS:
> You have a grown-up son, don't you?
795 > If you take our advice,
> you will send him to take your place.

STREPSIADES:
> Yes, I've a son, a refined, lovely lad.
> But he's not interested in higher education. What else can I do?

CHORUS:
> He's your son, is he not? Who is master of your house?

STREPSIADES:
800 > Well, he's a passionate, spirited boy from a fine family,
> the house of Coesyra, no less. But you're right, it's high time
> I set him straight, and if he says no, then he's out on his ear
> once and for all. Wait for me, I won't be long.

> *(Exit Strepsiades as the chorus serenades Socrates.)*

CHORUS:
> *Now it is clear, once and for all*
805 > *The great benefits we bring to you,*
> *For this man is at your beck and call*
> *To us alone, your prayers are due.*

> *You've created one hysterical man,*
810 > *His excitement cannot be contained.*
> *Now quickly take him for all you can*
> *For luck can change and drain away.*

> *(Enter Pheidippides, chased by Strepsiades.)*

STREPSIADES:
> Get out! By Vapor, out of my house, once and for all.
815 > Go and eat your Uncle Megacles out of house and home!

PHEIDIPPIDES:
> Father, whatever is the matter?
> You are clearly insane, by Zeus!

STREPSIADES:
> Listen to you, "By Zeus!" How childish!
> Fancy believing in Olympian Zeus at your age.

PHEIDIPPIDES:
  What on earth is so funny?   820

STREPSIADES:
  You are, a young child like you with such old-fashioned ideas,
  it's really quite ridiculous. But listen, come here, I want to reveal
      something to you. When you understand, then, and only then,
      my son,
  will you truly be a man. But you must ensure that no one else
      knows this.

PHEIDIPPIDES:
  Well, I'm here. Now what is it?   825

STREPSIADES:
  Did you or did you not just swear to Zeus?

PHEIDIPPIDES:
  I did.

STREPSIADES:
  Now you'll see the benefits of education.
  Pheidippides, there is no Zeus!

PHEIDIPPIDES:
  What!

STREPSIADES:
  Zeus is overthrown! Basin is king now!

PHEIDIPPIDES:
  Ha! What rot!

STREPSIADES:
  It's the truth.

PHEIDIPPIDES:
  I don't believe you. Who told you this nonsense?

STREPSIADES:
  Socrates the Melian[69] and Chaerephon,   830
  and he's an expert in the true path of . . . fleas.

---

69. Diagoras of Melos was condemned to death for his atheism and scorn for traditional religion.

PHEIDIPPIDES:
Oh dear, your insanity is at a really advanced stage
if you have begun to follow the views of those maniacs.

STREPSIADES:
How dare you say such things! These are brilliant men
835   with superb minds. They live a simple frugal life and refuse
to cut their hair, use soap, or set foot in a bathhouse.
But you, you've been taking yourself and my money to the
   cleaners for years, scrubbing away as if I was dead and buried!
Come on, hurry up, you have to go and learn in my place.

PHEIDIPPIDES:
What for? There's nothing even vaguely useful they could teach
840   me.

STREPSIADES:
Nothing useful? What about all worldly knowledge, eh?
You could start off by learning what an imbecile you are.
Hang on, I've just had a thought. Wait here!

(Exit Strepsiades.)

PHEIDIPPIDES:
Dear me! Father is clearly completely deranged. What should I do?
845   I could have him tried in court and found legally incompetent,[70]
or perhaps I had better book the undertaker right away.

(Enter Strepsiades holding two very similar-looking chickens.)

STREPSIADES:
Now then, tell me what you would call this.

PHEIDIPPIDES:
A chicken.

STREPSIADES:
Very good. And what would you call this?

(Strepsiades holds up the other chicken.)

---

70. According to Xenophon, *Memorabilia* 1.2.49, Socrates was accused of encouraging the young to use a law of this sort against their fathers but he was in fact opposed to it.

PHEIDIPPIDES:
  A chicken.

STREPSIADES:
  Really? You would call them both by the same name, eh?
  Now you really are being stupid. Here let me show you
  so you will know next time you are asked; this one here   850
  is indeed called a "chicken" . . . but this is a "chickeness."

PHEIDIPPIDES:
  "Chickeness"! Is that an example of the "worldly knowledge"
  you learned in that house of stupid old clods?

STREPSIADES:
  It is, but son, I couldn't remember most of the stuff they taught.
  Every time I learned something I would forget it. I'm just too old
      and . . .   855

PHEIDIPPIDES:
  That's why you've lost the clothes off your back, is it?

STREPSIADES:
  They're not lost, just donated to my educational endowment.

PHEIDIPPIDES:
  And just where are your shoes, you gullible old idiot?

STREPSIADES:
  To quote Pericles, "They were spent on necessary expenses."[71]
  Come on, let's go. Do this one thing for your father, even if you 860
  don't agree with it. I remember when you were a little six-year-
      old.
  Your little lisping voice begged me for a new toy cart as your
      festival
  present, and I spent my first hard-earned obol of jury pay on
      you.[72]

PHEIDIPPIDES:
  Oh, all right then, but you'll regret this.   865

---

71. Pericles apparently used ten talents of state funds to bribe the Spartans to with-
draw from Athenian territory in 445 B.C.E. He listed this in his annual accounts
presented to the Assembly as "payment for necessary expenses."

72. Jurors received three obols a day in payment for jury service.

STREPSIADES:

> Good lad, I knew you'd be persuaded. Socrates! Come out, come
> here!

>> *(Enter Socrates.)*

> Here is my son, as promised. I persuaded him to come along,
> though he was dead set against it at first.

SOCRATES:

> No, no, no, he simply will not do, he's a mere child. He would
> never
> get the hang of the way we tackle things here. He just wouldn't
> grasp it.

PHEIDIPPIDES:

870   Grasp your own tackle and then and go and hang yourself!

STREPSIADES:

> Pheidippides! Watch your language in front of the teacher!

SOCRATES:

> "Graaasp?" Just listen to his infantile diction!
> What ever do you expect me to do with such flaccid lips?
> How could he learn prevarication, incrimination, and
875   misrepresentation? Then again, for the right course fees
> it may be possible. Just look what a talent bought for
>   Hyperbolus![73]

STREPSIADES:

> You can do it! He'll learn, he's a natural, you'll find out!
> You should have seen him when he was a little lad. Gifted!
> A boy genius! He'd build the most beautiful mud pies, carve
880   little boats, and make toy chariots out of old shoes, and you can't
> even begin to imagine the inventive little frogs he made from
> pomegranates. I want you to teach him those two Arguments,
> the Superior, whatever that is, and the Inferior, you know, the one
> that can argue a wrongful case and defeat the Superior Argument.
> If you can't manage both, then at least make him learn the wrong
885   one.

---

73. The huge sum of money demanded for Hyperbolus' training is a comic indi-
cation of the amount of work it took to turn him into a presentable orator.

SOCRATES:
  He can learn it from the Arguments themselves. I must be off.

  (Exit Socrates.)

STREPSIADES:
  Remember, he needs to argue his way out of all types of legitimate
    lawsuits!

  (Enter the Superior Argument.)

SUPERIOR:
  Come out, let the audience have a look at you!
  You know how much you like to show off.   890

  (Enter the Inferior Argument.)

INFERIOR:
  Oh "get you hence,"[74] dear. *(He sees the audience.)* Ohhh! What a
    crowd,
  the more to witness your thrashing, the better. I just love it!

SUPERIOR:
  And who are you to think you can thrash me?

INFERIOR:
  Just an argument.

SUPERIOR:
  An Inferior Argument.

INFERIOR:
  Oh, aren't you the high and mighty one! That may be so darling,
  but I'll still thrash you all the same.   895

SUPERIOR:
  Really? And just how do you plan to do that?

INFERIOR:
  With innovative new ideas.

SUPERIOR:
  Oh very chic. You're very fashionable, aren't you,
  thanks to these idiots. *(Indicating the audience.)*

---

74. A quote from Euripides' play *Telephus*. See 922 note.

INFERIOR:
On the contrary, they are of the highest intelligence.

SUPERIOR:
I'm going to annihilate you.

INFERIOR:
I see. How?

SUPERIOR:
900   Simply by stating my just argument.

INFERIOR:
Then let me start by defeating it with a counterargument,
because it is quite clear that Justice doesn't exist.

SUPERIOR:
Don't be ridiculous!

INFERIOR:
Well, where is she then?

SUPERIOR:
She resides with the gods on Olympus, as well you know.[75]

INFERIOR:
Well then, if Justice lives on Olympus,
905   why hasn't Zeus been punished for locking up his father, mmm?[76]

SUPERIOR:
You're just spewing vileness. Urghh! Get me a bucket, someone!

INFERIOR:
You're a doddering old relic.

SUPERIOR:
And you take it up the ass!

INFERIOR:
What a rosy compliment!

SUPERIOR:
910   Freeloader!

---

75. Hesiod, *Works and Days* 257–259.
76. See *Euthyphro* 5e5–6a3 and note.

INFERIOR:
    You crown me with lilies!

SUPERIOR:
    Father beater!

INFERIOR:
    You're completely unaware that you're showering me with gold.

SUPERIOR:
    In my day, you'd be showered with lead.

INFERIOR:
    Yes, I know, but my dear fellow, in these modern times we
        live in,
    all your worse name-calling just pays me greater honor!

SUPERIOR:
    You're completely brazen!

INFERIOR:
    And you are absolutely archaic!   915

SUPERIOR:
    It's your fault that the youth of today refuses
    to attend school. You'll get your comeuppance.
    You'll see. The Athenians will realize what fools
    they've been to learn their lessons from the likes of you!

INFERIOR:
    Pooh! You need to freshen up a bit.   920

SUPERIOR:
    Oh, you've been busy all right, you worthless beggar.
    You used to be Telephus the Mysian,
    gnawing on old Pendeletean sayings from a tatty old swag bag.[77]

INFERIOR:
    How shrewd . . .

---

77. The central character of Euripides' tragedy *Telephus*, staged in 438 B.C.E. He
was king of Mysia (in the northwest of Asia Minor), but appeared on stage as a
beggar dressed in rags. Pandeletus was a politician and an aggressive prosecutor
with an odious reputation.

SUPERIOR:

925   How insane . . .

INFERIOR:

                . . . all that you've said I've done.

SUPERIOR:

                                . . . the city is to support you,
        as you corrupt its young.

INFERIOR:

        Don't even think about trying to teach this boy,
        you crusty old Cronus!

SUPERIOR:

930   It is my duty. He needs to be saved from
        the threat of spouting senseless gibberish.

INFERIOR:

        (To Pheidippides.) Come over here and ignore this reactionary old
            maniac.

SUPERIOR:

        Keep away from him or you'll be sorry!

CHORUS:

        Oh, stop all this fighting and arguing!

            (Addressing the Superior Argument.)

935   Why don't you give an account of the schooling
        you used to give in the old days,

            (Addressing the Inferior Argument.)

                                and then you
        can tell us about your new educational methods.
        Then this boy can hear your conflicting arguments,
        make his own mind up, and enroll in the school of his choice.

SUPERIOR:

        I see no reason why not.

INFERIOR:

        I'm happy to do it.

CHORUS:
Good. Who would like to speak first?   940

INFERIOR:
Oh, let him go first.
I want to hear what he has to say.
Then I'm going to let my innovative phraseology fly
and shoot down his arguments once and for all.
My penetrating insights are like hornets,   945
and they'll prick him blind.
And if I hear so much as a peep out of him,
he'll wish he was dead and buried!

CHORUS:
Now our two antagonists
will decide which one is cleverest.   950
The cut and thrust of confrontation,
a war of words and machination.
This ideological contest
will decide which one is best.
The end result of this demonstration   955
is the very future of education!
You crowned the older generation with your morality.
Now is your chance to proudly tell us exactly what you stand for.   960

SUPERIOR:
Then let me begin by explaining how education was run in the
     good old days
when my just cause was predominant and discretion was the
     aspiration of every man.
First, it was a given that boys should be seen and not heard and
     that students
should attend their district schools marching through the streets in
     orderly pairs
behind the lyre master. Moreover, they were never allowed to wear
     cloaks,   965
even if the snow was falling as thick as porridge. These boys were
     then taught fine
patriotic songs and not to rub their thighs together while seated in
     the classroom!

Ah yes, what stirring hymns they would sing: "City-destroying
  Pallas" and "Hark I hear
a far-off tune," and they sung strong and proud like the manly
  fathers who raised them.
And if any boy engaged in classroom buffoonery or attempted to
970   torture the music
by singing in the cacophonic, newfangled style of that awful lyre
  plucker Phrynis,[78]
he was given a damned good thrashing for deliberately perverting
  the Muses!
Also, while sitting in the gymnasium the boys had to keep their
  legs closed in order
that they not expose the spectators to any inappropriate and
  offensive sights.
When they stood up, they had to smooth the sand down where
975   they were sitting
so that they would not leave behind any untoward impressions of
  their manhood.
No boy was permitted to oil himself below the waist, and
  consequently each
had a lovely soft down on his balls like a pair of fresh ripe
  apricots . . .
They were not permitted to entice older lovers with effeminate
  voices
or seductive looks, or mince around pimping themselves out to all
980   and sundry!
No taking the radish head during dinner, or grabbing an elder's
  celery stick
or pulling his parsley. No nibbling on tit-bits, no giggling at the
  table, no sitting with legs crossed, no . . .

INFERIOR:
  What a load of archaic claptrap! Your speech, sir, reeks of rotten
    old Dipolieic beef.[79]

---

78. An important figure in the development of the new music of Aristophanes'
day.

79. This refers to the Buphonia, the sacred sacrifice of a bull to Zeus Polieus
("protector of the city") as part of the Diplolieia festival.

It is crawling with grasshoppers and hums to the antiquated strains
  of Cedeides![80]   985

SUPERIOR:
  Clearly you are missing the point. It was my system of student
    tutoring that raised
  the men who fought so bravely at Marathon.[81] All you do is train
    our young to be ashamed
  of themselves and hide behind their cloaks. It grieves me to watch
    the war dance
  at the Panathenaea and to have to see these wimpy lads who can
    barely lift a shield,
  embarrassed at the sight of their own manly meat![82] It's a disgrace
    to Athena herself!   990
  So come on, young fellow, the choice is clear: choose me, the
    Superior Argument.
  I'll teach you to detest hanging about in the marketplace and to
    keep out of public baths.
  You'll learn to be ashamed of the shameful and to burn with
    indignation when you are ridiculed.
  You'll gracefully let your elders and betters have your seat, and you
    will always treat your
  parents with the utmost respect. You will do nothing to harm your
    personal virtue.   995
  No more chasing in and out of party girls' bedrooms and running
    the risk of ruining your
  reputation because of some harlot's love tokens. No more arguing
    with your father,
  nor insulting his status by calling him a "crusty old fart" or
    "Cronus' older brother."
  No, you'll come to respect all those years he spent raising you from
    a tiny little chick.

---

80. Golden grasshoppers (cicadas), worn by the older generation, were a symbol
of the Athenians' origins from the earth of Attica. Cedeides was a poet–musician
who composed in an "old-fashioned" style.

81. A famous Athenian victory over a vastly superior Persian force in 490 B.C.E.

82. Because they don't train regularly in the gymnasium, they are unused to being
naked in public.

INFERIOR:
    Oh dear me, "young fellow," if you take his advice, by Dionysus,
1000   you'll turn out
    like those dullard sons of Hippocrates[83] and be forever known as a
    little milksop.

SUPERIOR:
    Don't listen to him. You'll be forever in the wrestling school, your
      bronzed body
    glistening and hard. No wasting precious time twittering away on
      absurd topics
    in the marketplace, nor bickering in the courts, splitting hairs,
      arguing the toss
    and wrangling over some insignificant little suit. We'll see you at
1005   the Academy,[84]
    bravely racing a friend under the boughs of holy olive trees, your
      hair festooned
    with fresh-cut reeds, surrounded by sweet-scented wildflowers as
      the catkins
    gently fall from the willows. There, you'll not have a care in the
      world, as the trees
    rustle gently in the balmy breeze and you partake of the joys of
      spring.
1010   This is the right way for you, my lad, and if you do what I say
    you'll be eternally blessed
    with a strapping body, a gleaming complexion,
    huge shoulders, a tiny little tongue,
    big buttocks, and a small cock.[85]
1015   Should you choose to follow the fashion currently
    in vogue among the young men of this city,
    then it'll be pasty skin, round shoulders,

---

83. Hippocrates was elected to the Athenian generalship in 426–425 B.C.E. He died at the battle of Delium in 424 B.C.E., leaving three sons, Demophon, Pericles, and Telesippus, who were regarded as uneducated morons by the comic playwrights.

84. A public park about a mile from the city, dedicated to the hero Academos. It was later to become famous as the site of Plato's school.

85. 1010–1014 are a vivid description of the "ideal" male form in Athenian art to the mid-fifth century B.C.E. Small uncircumcised penises were the aesthetic ideal in young men.

concave chest, an enormous tongue,
no ass, a great hunk of meat, and a very long ... turn of phrase!
He will have you believe that what should be shameful
is beautiful, and what should be beautiful is made shameful!   1020
Worst of all, in no time at all he'll turn you into an ass bandit
like that lecherous old queen, Antimachus.[86]

CHORUS:

> *(Addressing the Superior Argument.)*

> *Such elevated sentiments*   1025
> *Extolling high accomplishments,*
> *Presenting such a fine defense*
> *In praise of pride and sound good sense.*
> *What blessed men you once did raise*
> *Before our time, in olden days.*   1030

> *(Addressing the Inferior Argument.)*

> *So be creative with your modern art.*
> *This man has made a very good start.*

If you want to avoid looking completely foolish and win this
   argument,
then I think you had better use some of your crafty techniques.   1035

INFERIOR:
In point of fact, I've been standing here for quite some time
literally busting a gut to confound his ridiculous statements
with my "counterintelligence." Why else do you think the
   philosophers
named me the Inferior Argument? Because it was I who created
the concept of disputing entrenched ideals and ethics.   1040
My dear boy, don't you see? To be able to take up the Inferior
   Argument and win
is worth far, far more than any number of silver coins you could
   care to count.
Let's examine these educational methods that he regards with such
   great confidence.
First of all, I clearly heard him say that he would abolish all bathing
   in warm water.

---

86. Otherwise unknown.

Tell me, sir, if you will, the basis for your belief that hot baths are
1045   bad.

SUPERIOR:
    That they are most reprehensible and make the men who take
        them effeminate!

INFERIOR:
    I've got you! You're quite pinned down and there's no escape!
    Now tell me this, which son of Zeus do you believe has the finest
    spirit and had successfully undertaken the most labors?

SUPERIOR:
1050   As far as I am concerned, there is no better man than Heracles.[87]

INFERIOR:
    Precisely! And have you ever seen a cold Heraclean bath?[88]
    And who could possibly be more manly than Heracles?

SUPERIOR:
    That's exactly why the gymnasiums are empty, because the youth
    of today are all at the bathhouses spouting this kind of claptrap!

INFERIOR:
    Next, you take exception to our youngsters frequenting the public
1055   marketplace,
    whereas I wholeheartedly recommend it. After all, if meeting in
        public is so appalling,
    why does Homer describe Nestor and other men of wisdom as
        "public speakers"?
    Let me now take up the issue of the tongue, which he states is not
        seemly for
    the young to exercise. I have to disagree and am of the opposite
        opinion.
    In addition, he pronounces that one must be discreet, a pair of fatal
1060   assumptions.
    I would dearly love for you to tell me anyone who gained the
        slightest benefit
    from behaving discreetly. Just name them and prove me wrong.

---

87. See *Euthyphro* 4a11 note.

88. Natural warm springs that, according to legend, were a gift from the craftsman
god Hephaestus to Heracles.

SUPERIOR:

There's plenty. What about Peleus?[89] He won a knife for his
    discretion.

INFERIOR:

A knife! What a delightful little thing to earn, by Zeus!
Even Hyperbolus, who's made a heap of cash swindling us all   1065
    at the lamp market, can't boast that he ever earned a knife!

SUPERIOR:

Thanks to his discretion, Peleus won the right to marry Thetis.

INFERIOR:

Yes, a little too discreet between the sheets, I heard. That's why
she ran out on him, because he simply wasn't outrageous enough
    in bed.[90]
You know some women like it that way, you horny old Cronus
    stud!   1070
Just consider, dear boy, what a life of discretion consists of
and all the hedonistic delights you would miss out on—boys, girls,
drinking games, fancy food, fine wine, a good laugh.
How on earth could you endure life without these necessities?
Now, let us move on and discuss the needs of human nature.   1075
Suppose that you've been indulging in an illicit love affair. You are
    discovered!
A scandal! What will you do? You are finished, because you don't
    have the means
to argue your way out of trouble. But if you choose to make my
    acquaintance,
your nature can run free, with a spring in your step and a smile on
    your face,
and shameful thoughts will never even cross your mind. If the
    husband accuses you   1080
of adultery, plead innocence and blame Zeus. Say that clearly he
    can't resist his lust

---

89. The father of Achilles. He was falsely accused of rape and banished to Mount
Pelion to be the prey of wild beasts. The gods took pity on him and sent him a
knife for protection.

90. Thetis, a goddess, was the mother of Achilles. One myth has her leaving
Peleus because he rebuked her severely.

for women, so how can you, a mere mortal, be expected to have
more strength than a god?

SUPERIOR:
Yes, but what if he takes your advice and gets punished by pubic
plucking, scrotal singeing,
and a jolly good rectal radish ramming?[91] No argument of yours is
going to help him after that!

INFERIOR:
You mean people might think that he liked having his asshole
1085   spread wide?

SUPERIOR:
Yes, what could possibly be worse than that?

INFERIOR:
Will you concede to me if I can prove this point to you?

SUPERIOR:
If you can, you'll not hear another peep out of me.

INFERIOR:
How would you describe most of our lawyers?

SUPERIOR:
1090   They're wide asses.

INFERIOR:
Quite right, and what about our tragic dramatists?

SUPERIOR:
All wide asses.

INFERIOR:
Yes, indeed. And our politicians?

SUPERIOR:
Definitely wide asses.

INFERIOR:
Then surely you must see that you are defending a lost cause.
1095   I mean, take a good look at the audience.
What would you call most of them?

---

91. Punishments legally available to cuckolded men.

SUPERIOR:
I'm looking.

INFERIOR:
And what do you see?

SUPERIOR:
By all the gods, most of them are . . . wide asses!

(He starts pointing at individual members of the audience.)

Well I know he is, and he definitely is,
and that long-haired chap over there and . . . oh my!   1100

INFERIOR:
Well then, what have you got to say for yourself now?

SUPERIOR:
I have to admit that you butt fuckers
have beaten me.
Here, take my cloak.
I think I might give it a try myself!

(Exit Superior Argument.)

INFERIOR:
(To Strepsiades.) Well then, what do you think? Are you and your
son going to run off home,   1105
or are you going to leave the boy with me to learn my oratorical
arts?

STREPSIADES:
He's all yours to teach, and you have my permission to beat him
too.
Remember, I want him to have a razor-sharp tongue and fully
adjustable too, with one edge honed for petty lawsuits and the
other
sharpened for cutting to the chase on more serious matters.   1110

INFERIOR:
Have no fear. He will return an expert in sophistry.

PHEIDIPPIDES:
I'll return a pasty-faced fiend, you mean!

CHORUS:
Go on, off you go.

(Exit Inferior Argument and Pheidippides into the Pondertorium.)

I think that one day you may well
rue the day you did this.

(Exit Strepsiades.)

1115   It's time to tell the judges why we should have first prize,[92]
and why honoring this Cloud chorus will prove extremely wise.
When you're plowing all your fields and you reach the sowing
    date,
we'll rain on your land first and make the others wait.
What's more, we'll watch your vines and carefully guard your
    crops.
1120   We'll stop them getting parched and swamped by huge raindrops.
But if, on the other hand, you mortals treat us with disrespect,
we goddesses will shower you with our malicious effects.
Your lands will yield you nothing, your wine cellars deplete,
for your olives and your grapes will be pelted by our sleet.
1125   When we see you baking bricks and laying tiles of clay,
we'll crack them with our hail, then wash them all away.
Should a friend or family member happen to be wed,
We'll blow a gale all night and keep him from his bed.
You'd rather be in Egypt sizzling in the desert sun,
1130   Than make an unfair judgment and not vote us number one!

(Enter Strepsiades.)

STREPSIADES:
Let's see now; five, four, three, two . . . oh no, only two more days
until the old–and–new day at the end of the month,[93] the day I fear
the most, the day that makes me tremble, the day that gives me the
    jitters,
the day that debts are due! Every last one of my creditors will
    have

---

92. Plays were presented as part of a dramatic competition in honor of the god
Dionysus and were judged by a panel of citizens.
93. See 617 note.

paid their court fees[94] and are planning to destroy me, once and
   for all!   1135
They won't listen: I've pleaded with them to give me more time,
   begged
to have my credit extended, implored them to write off my debts.
But nothing works. They all want paying. They just call me a
   criminal,
hurl abuse, and threaten me with the law! The unfeeling bastards!

   (He walks toward the stage left door.)

Well, let them try it, that's what I say, they can take me to court   1140
for all I care. They'll be sorry, if my Pheidippides has learned how
to talk the talk. Well, there's only one way to find out. I'll give the
Pondertorium a knock and see if he's ready.

   (Strepsiades knocks on the door.)

Boy! Boy! Open up! Boy!

   (Enter Socrates.)

SOCRATES:
Ah, Strepsiades, good day to you.   1145

STREPSIADES:
Likewise, mate! I've brought you a little gift here.

   (Strepsiades hands Socrates a small bag of barley.)[95]

It's right and proper to bring a present for the teacher.
Has my lad learned the argument, you know, the one
that did that little turn for us a while ago?

SOCRATES:
Indeed he has.

STREPSIADES:
Oh, Mistress of Misrepresentation, how marvelous!   1150

SOCRATES:
Now you will be able to contest all the litigation you please.

---

94. To register proceedings against a debtor.

95. All he can afford, given his debts, or perhaps all the frugal Socrates accepts (see
835).

STREPSIADES:
  What? Even if a witness swore that they saw me borrow the cash?

SOCRATES:
  Even if there were a thousand witnesses!

  (Strepsiades breaks into a joyous song.)

STREPSIADES:
  Then be it known, let my shouts attest
1155 *That all the moneylenders have cause to mourn,*
  For I banish your debts and compound interest.
  I've no more need to endure your scorn.

  For today my prodigy has sprung
  From within these very walls
1160 *Armed with a glinting two-edged tongue*
  To save my house and foes forestall.

  So run and fetch him with a shout,
  He will relieve his father's woes.
1165 *Call my child, have him come out,*
  Come forth, my son, it is time to go.

  (Enter Pheidippides.)

SOCRATES:
  I believe this is the man you are looking for.

STREPSIADES:
  My dear boy! My dear, dear boy!

SOCRATES:
  Take him and be on your way.

  (Exit Socrates.)

STREPSIADES:
1170 My son! My child!
  Hooray! Hooray!
  Just let me look at you! What a lovely skin tone!⁹⁶

---

96. Presumably the actor playing Pheidippides has changed his mask and now resembles the students met at line 133, with a pallid complexion and gaunt features.

I can see the contention and the negation written all over your
    face.
You look like a true Athenian now, with our characteristic "I've no
    idea
what you're talking about" look blooming in your cheeks. Why,
    you've even
picked up the look-of-righteous-indignation-even-when-you're-
    in-the-wrong expression.   1175
Now you can save me, since it was you who got me into this mess
    in the first place.

PHEIDIPPIDES:
  What are you are so afraid of?

STREPSIADES:
  Why, the old-and-new day, of course!

PHEIDIPPIDES:
  Are you trying to tell me that there's a day that's both old and new?

STREPSIADES:
  Of course there is! It's the day when my creditors will file their
    court deposits.   1180

PHEIDIPPIDES:
  Then they'll lose their money, won't they? There's no way that one
    day
  can suddenly become two days, is there?

STREPSIADES:
  Isn't there?

PHEIDIPPIDES:
  Of course not. I mean that's like saying that a single woman could
    be both
  a young girl and an old woman at exactly the same time.

STREPSIADES:
  But it's the law.   1185

PHEIDIPPIDES:
  No, no, no. They've obviously completely misconstrued the law.

STREPSIADES:
  What does the law really mean, then?

PHEIDIPPIDES:
Solon,[97] the elder statesman, was essentially a benefactor of the
people, correct?

STREPSIADES:
What's that got to do with the old-and-new day?

PHEIDIPPIDES:
He was the one who decreed that there should be two days
1190 set aside for the issuing of court summonses, and all deposits
must be lodged on the new day.

STREPSIADES:
Then why did he add the old day too?

PHEIDIPPIDES:
My dear fellow, to give the accused the opportunity to settle out of
court
one day prior to their scheduled trials. Then they would avoid
harassment
1195 by their creditors until the actual morning of the new day.[98]

STREPSIADES:
If that's the case, why do the court officials receive deposits on the
old and new day instead of just on the new day?

PHEIDIPPIDES:
Isn't it obvious? They're double-dipping.
They're just like the festival taste testers
1200 filching a foretaste of the fees as fast as is feasible!

STREPSIADES:
Ha ha! You poor fools! You don't stand a chance! Look at you
simpletons sitting

---

97. Solon was a sixth-century Athenian statesman, lawgiver, and poet. He abol-
ished the practice of placing a free man in slavery for the nonpayment of debts. He
was widely regarded as the founding father of the Athenian constitution.

98. Pheidippides uses his new education to twist the meaning of the old-and-new
day. He explains that the old day was set aside for settlements, whereas on the new
day the debts were actually due. He therefore disputes the validity of a system that
marks one day for the collection of debts. Strepsiades, suitably befuddled, asks why
the courts are allowed to collect on two separate days (the old *and* new day), and
Pheidippides replies that they are obviously cheating, which makes any claims
against his father through the courts invalid.

Out there, just begging to be ripped off by us members of the
     intelligentsia!
You're dunderheads, clods, and empty vessels, nothing but a herd
     of sheep!
It is time I serenaded this splendid good fortune
with a nice hymn in honor of me and my son.   1205

          (Strepsiades breaks into song.)

"O Strepsiades, you are the lucky one
So fortunate and so wise,
You've raised a fine, upstanding son."
Thus my friends will eulogize.

When they find out I have a winner,   1210
You'll see the jealousy on their faces.
So let's celebrate with a great big dinner
Before you argue all my cases.

          (Exit Strepsiades and Pheidippides. Enter First Creditor and a
          witness.)

FIRST CREDITOR:
     So what's a man supposed to do, throw his own money down the
          drain?
     Not likely, I shouldn't have felt so embarrassed, I should have just
          said no   1215
     right when he asked me for the loan. Then I wouldn't be in this
          mess.

          (Addressing the witness.)

     And I wouldn't have to waste your time dragging you all the way
          down here
     to witness a summons for money that was rightfully mine in the
          first place.
     Both ways I lose, either my money or the goodwill of a neighbor.
     It's no good worrying about it; I have my duty as a true Athenian, 1220
     I must go to court. I hereby summon Strepsiades to appear in . . .

          (Enter Strepsiades.)

STREPSIADES:
     Who is it?

FIRST CREDITOR:
>   ...in court on the old-and-new day.

STREPSIADES:
>   Did you hear that? He's summoned me on two different days.
>   Why, pray, are you summoning me?

FIRST CREDITOR:
1225
>   You owe me twelve hundred drachmas. You borrowed
>   the money to purchase that dapple-gray horse.[99]

STREPSIADES:
>   A horse! Did you hear that? Everyone knows that I can't stand
>   horses.

FIRST CREDITOR:
>   You made a sacred oath before the gods that you would repay me.

STREPSIADES:
>   Indeed I did, but you see, that was before my lad Pheidippides
>   had gone and learned the unbeatable Argument.

FIRST CREDITOR:
>   I see, and I suppose now you think you can simply forgo your
1230
>   debts?

STREPSIADES:
>   Don't you think it's reasonable that I receive some benefit from his
>   education?

FIRST CREDITOR:
>   Well then, if that's the way you want it. Are you willing to refute
>   your oath before the gods while standing on sacred ground?

STREPSIADES:
>   Which particular gods?

FIRST CREDITOR:
>   Zeus, Hermes,[100] and Poseidon.

STREPSIADES:
1235
>   Of course! I'd even pay three obols for the privilege.

---

99. See line 23.

100. The messenger god, son of Zeus and a nymph.

(The First Creditor is shocked and angry, becoming agitated and animated.)

FIRST CREDITOR:
By all the gods! May you be damned for your blasphemy!

(Strepsiades grabs hold of the First Creditor and pats him on the belly.)

STREPSIADES:
You know if we were to split you open and rub you down
with salt, your belly would make a lovely wineskin.

FIRST CREDITOR:
How dare you!

STREPSIADES:
It'd hold at least four jugs' worth.[101]

FIRST CREDITOR:
By Zeus almighty, by all the gods, you'll never get away with
this!   1240

STREPSIADES:
Ha, ha! That's a good one, that is, "by all the gods!" Don't make
me laugh!
Those of us "in the know" realize that Zeus is just a joke.

FIRST CREDITOR:
I'm telling you, soon enough, you'll pay for this. Just tell me one
thing.
Do you have any intention of paying what you owe me?

STREPSIADES:
Hang on, I'll let you know . . .   1245

(Strepsiades runs off.)

FIRST CREDITOR:
(To the witness.) What's he up to now? Do you reckon he's going to
pay me?

(Strepsiades comes out again holding a meal kneader.)

---

101. See 641–645.

STREPSIADES:

Where's that man demanding money? Right then, tell me what
this is.

FIRST CREDITOR:

That? It's a meal kneader, of course.

STREPSIADES:

And you have the gall to ask me for money! How could you be so
stupid?

1250   You won't catch me parting with a single obol to such a moron.
You're the one who "needs the fee." It's obviously a "fe-meal
kneader."

(Strepsiades tries to dismiss the First Creditor.)

FIRST CREDITOR:

I take it that you have no intention of paying your debt.

STREPSIADES:

Not likely. Now turn around, get off my doorstep, go on, piss off!

FIRST CREDITOR:

I will go, straight to the court to lodge my deposit. I'll see you
1255   prosecuted if it's the last thing I do!

(Exit First Creditor and Witness.)

STREPSIADES:

You'll just be adding that to those twelve hundred drachmas and
increasing
your losses. Will you people never learn?
I feel sorry for him really. I mean, imagine not knowing your
gender!

(Enter Second Creditor.)

SECOND CREDITOR:

Oh no! No!

STREPSIADES:

Ah!
1260   What now! Who the blazes is this chap, warbling dirges?
Could it be one of Carcinus' daimons making that sound?[102]

---

102. Carcinus was a tragic playwright who won a first prize in 446 B.C.E.

SECOND CREDITOR:
Why do you care to know my name? I am doomed, doomed!

STREPSIADES:
Well go and be doomed somewhere else, will you!

SECOND CREDITOR:
O heartless daimons, o calamity that destroyed my chariot!
O Pallas Athena, you have brought me rack and ruin![103]   1265

STREPSIADES:
The true tragedy is how you're mutilating those lines.

SECOND CREDITOR:
You may mock me, sir, but all I want is for your son to repay
the money that he borrowed from me, particularly in light
of my recent hapless misadventure.

STREPSIADES:
What money?   1270

SECOND CREDITOR:
The money I lent him.

STREPSIADES:
Oh dear, I can see that you're in a bit of a mess.

SECOND CREDITOR:
I was rounding a bend and fell out of my chariot.

STREPSIADES:
Out of your mind, more like! I think you're the one who's
"round the bend," coming here spouting gibberish.

SECOND CREDITOR:
It is not gibberish. I just want to be repaid!

STREPSIADES:
You're clearly quite insane. A lost cause, I'm afraid.   1275

SECOND CREDITOR:
What do you mean?

---

103. These lines parody a speech in a tragedy by Carcinus' son, Xenocles.

STREPSIADES:
I believe you have been knocked senseless; your brain's addled.

SECOND CREDITOR:
And I believe I'll be seeing you in court, by Hermes,
if you don't pay me back the money that I'm owed!

STREPSIADES:
Tell me something. When Zeus makes it rain, do you believe that he sends
fresh water each time or that the sun absorbs the moisture from the
1280   earth,
reclaims it, and sends it back down again in the form of a rain
shower?[104]

SECOND CREDITOR:
I have absolutely no idea, and I don't see what it has to do with . . .

STREPSIADES:
Well, how can you justify reclaiming your money if you
don't understand the rudiments of meteorology?

SECOND CREDITOR:
1285   Listen, if you can't handle the whole payment this month,
then how about just paying me the interest?

STREPSIADES:
What do you mean, "interest"? I'm not in the least bit interested in
your problems.

SECOND CREDITOR:
I mean the charge on the loan that increases in size
from day to day and month to month as time flows on by.

STREPSIADES:
1290   That's all very well, but do you think the sea
has increased in size at all since olden times?

SECOND CREDITOR:
By Zeus, of course not. It would be against
the law of nature for the sea to change in size.

_____

104. A parody of various philosophers' views.

STREPSIADES:

Well then, you pitiful wretch, if the sea doesn't increase in size
with all the rivers flowing into it, who the blazes do you think
you are to try and increase the size of your loan? Now bugger off   1295
away from my house, or you'll get a damn good prodding!

(Strepsiades calls inside his house.)

Boy! Bring me my cattle prod!

(A slave rushes out with a cattle prod.)

SECOND CREDITOR:

Help! Somebody witness this!

(Strepsiades starts prodding the Second Creditor.)

STREPSIADES:

Giddy up! Get up there! Get going before I brand your horse's ass!

SECOND CREDITOR:

This is outrageous! I protest!

(Strepsiades continues his assault.)

STREPSIADES:

Giddy up! Move it! Or I'll make a gelding out of you!   1300

*(The Second Creditor flees offstage, and Strepsiades calls out after
him.)*

Oh, you can move quickly enough when you want to! You can
take your
horses and your chariot wheels and stick them where the sun don't
shine!

(Exit Strepsiades.)

CHORUS:

Depravity often proves a fatal attraction
That can drive an old man to distraction.
This one thinks he can evade his debts,   1305
So he'll push his luck and hedge his bets.
But we all know that one day soon,
There will come an end to this honeymoon,
That will force our sophist roughly back
From his latest wicked track.   1310

For he will discover presently
The consequences of his desperate plea.
For his son has learned the wily art
1315   *Of successfully arguing the unjust part.*
He defeats all opponents however strong
Even when his case is plainly wrong.
But I have a feeling that these disputes
1320   *Will make him wish that his son was mute!*

(Enter a disheveled Strepsiades.)

STREPSIADES:
Oh! Oh!
Help me! Friends, relatives, citizens, help!
Come quickly! I'm in terrible danger! Please!
I'm under attack, he's pummeling my head,
gashing my cheeks! Help me! Help me!

(Enter Pheidippides, looking very smug.)

STREPSIADES:
1325   You monster! You would dare to strike your own father?

PHEIDIPPIDES:
That's right, old man.

STREPSIADES:
You hear that? He even admits to it!

PHEIDIPPIDES:
Freely.

STREPSIADES:
You're despicable, a father beater and a criminal!

PHEIDIPPIDES:
Oh, say those things again, more, more.
You know how I just love to be insulted.

STREPSIADES:
1330   You filthy asshole!

PHEIDIPPIDES:
Please, keep showering me with roses.

STREPSIADES:
You would dare to raise a hand against your own father?

PHEIDIPPIDES:
Of course I would, by Zeus, and moreover I was perfectly
justified in giving you a beating as well.

STREPSIADES:
You little bugger! How can striking your own father ever be right?

PHEIDIPPIDES:
I'll prove it to you, by arguing my view, and I'll win too.

STREPSIADES:
You'll never win on this point. It's impossible!   1335

PHEIDIPPIDES:
On the contrary, it'll be a walkover. So, decide
which of the two Arguments you want to present.

STREPSIADES:
Which two Arguments?

PHEIDIPPIDES:
The Superior or Inferior.

STREPSIADES:
It's unbelievable, and to think it was I who had you
educated to argue successfully against Justice.
But there's absolutely no way you're going to be able   1340
to convince me that it is right for a son to beat his own father.

PHEIDIPPIDES:
Oh, but I shall convince you. In fact, you'll be so convinced once
    you've heard
me out, that you'll have nothing at all worthwhile to say on the
    matter.

STREPSIADES:
Go on then. Let's hear what you have to say for yourself. I can't
    wait.

CHORUS:
Old man, it's time you started thinking   1345
about what you need to say to win.
He would not be quite so arrogant
if he did not have an argument.
It is the reason for his insolence.   1350

CHORUS:

> Please tell the chorus how you came to be involved in this dispute.
> Tell us in your own words what actually happened.

STREPSIADES:

> Oh, I'll tell you all right. You'll hear every sordid detail of this
>   horrible squabble.
> We were inside enjoying a nice dinner when I asked him to fetch
>   his lyre
> and sing us an after-dinner song. I suggested he do a bit of "Hark
>   the Hallowed Ram
> Was Shorn" by Simonides,[105] but he would have none of it. No,
>   he told me that strumming
> a lyre and singing at dinner parties was "terribly passé" and said
>   that only old women
> grinding barley at the stone sing those kinds of songs anymore!

1355

PHEIDIPPIDES:

> Yes, and that explains why you received a thrashing. Who do you
>   think you are,
> ordering me to croon some monotonous old song like a chirping
>   grasshopper?

1360

STREPSIADES:

> That's exactly the kind of talk he was spouting inside, and what's
>   more,
> he even had the gall to announce that Simonides was a terrible
>   poet!
> I just couldn't believe my ears. Well, I swallowed my anger, for the
>   moment,
> and asked him ever so nicely to pick up the myrtle bough and
>   recite a little
> Aeschylus[106] for me, and do you know what he said? "Oh yes,
>   Aeschylus, surely
> the foremost of all poets at being loud, pompous, bombastic, and
>   inaccessible."
> Well, I nearly had a heart attack I was so angry at him, but yet
>   again, I curbed

1365

---

105. Simonides of Ceos (c. 556–468 B.C.E.), a prolific poet.

106. Aeschylus (525/4–456/5 B.C.E.) was one of the most famous and respected Athenian tragedians.

my fury and said calmly, "Why don't you come up with some of
    that clever
modern stuff, something from one of those fashionable poets
    you're always
going on about." And with that he blurted out some disgusting
    lines from Euripides,[107]   1370
about a brother and sister going at it together! Well, that was it, the
    last straw,
I could contain myself no longer, and I let him have it. I told him
just what I thought and it wasn't pretty either. What's more he
    answered
me back with some of the foulest language I have ever heard. At
    that moment
he leapt to his feet and weighed into me, first pushing and shoving.
    Then he grabbed   1375
my throat and started shaking me and punching and kicking. It
    was terrible!

PHEIDIPPIDES:
    I was well within my rights to punish you, after you dared to insult
    a gifted man like Euripides.

STREPSIADES:
    Gifted! He's just a . . . No, you'll only lay into me all over again.

PHEIDIPPIDES:
    And I'd be justified too, by Zeus!

STREPSIADES:
    How would you be justified? You insolent ruffian, have you
    forgotten who raised you?   1380
    I was the one who had to listen to your lisping baby talk when you
    went "wu-wu!"
    I knew what you wanted and would fetch you something to drink.
    Then you would go
    "foo-foo!" and daddy here would get you some bread. And when
    you cried "poo-poo!"
    it was me who would pick you up, take you outside, and let you
    do your little doo-doos!   1385

---

107. Euripides (485/47–407/6 B.C.E.), the tragic playwright, was a contemporary
of Aristophanes. The reference is probably to his play *Aeolus*.

But you, on the other hand, couldn't care less about my needs. Why just then, when you

were strangling me, I was completely ignored. Even though I was screaming that I was

about to shit my pants, you just kept right on throttling away. You literally squeezed

the crap out of me, and I did my poo-poo right there and then!

1390   It's a disgraceful way to treat your dear old dad.

CHORUS:

The hearts of the young are all a flutter
To hear what words this lad might utter
To justify such disrespect
Could ever be deemed correct
1395 *For such an outcome would surely mean*
That an old man's hide's not worth a bean!

Now, you mover and shaker, you maestro of modernity, it is your turn.

You must persuade him to accept your point of view.

PHEIDIPPIDES:

Let me first say how pleasurable it is to be acquainted with modern ways and intelligent

notions, for it enables one to disdain conventional practices from a
1400   superior vantage point.

When I filled my brain with only the mindless thoughts of horse riding I could hardly even blurt

out three words without making some stupid mistake. But thanks to my adversary here,

who saw to my education, I now possess a keen intellect and am proficient in finite conception,

subtle argument, and detailed contemplation. In effect, I believe I have the necessary skills

to fully demonstrate that it is perfectly justified to discipline one's
1405   own father.

STREPSIADES:

I wish you'd go back to your horses, by Zeus! I would much rather have to pay

for a four-horse chariot team than run the risk of sustaining bodily harm every day!

PHEIDIPPIDES:

If I may be allowed to return to the point in my argument from
where I was so rudely
interrupted. Tell me this, did you ever have occasion to beat me
when I was a child?

STREPSIADES:

Yes, but it was always for your own good. I had your best interests
at heart.   1410

PHEIDIPPIDES:

Then surely it is justified for me to beat you for your own good, if,
by your definition,
"having someone else's best interests at heart" means to beat them.
How is it justified
that your body should be protected against beatings but mine not?
Is it not true that we
are both freemen? "Suffer the little children, do you think the
father should not?"[108]
No doubt you will attempt to defend yourself by stating that it is
quite legitimate for   1415
this kind of punishment to be meted out to children, and yet, I
would say that the
elderly are living a "second childhood." This being the case, surely
it is only right
that the elderly should be chastised more severely than the young,
as they should
have certainly learned right and wrong after a lifetime of
experience.

STREPSIADES:

There's not a place in the world where it is legitimate for a son to
beat his father!   1420

PHEIDIPPIDES:

But it is men who make legislation, men just like you and me. In
past times,
one man simply persuaded another that this was the way things
should be.

---

108. An adaptation of Euripides, *Alcestis* 691. A son asks his father to die in his
place. The father replies, "You like the daylight; do you think your father doesn't?"

Therefore what is preventing me from similarly stating a new
     "law" for times to come
specifying that sons should be permitted to beat their fathers in
     return?
"This will now be retroactive legislation, and all claims for
     compensation for blows
1425
previously sustained will not be considered and shall hereby be
     stricken from the record."
Examine chickens and other such farmyard animals. You will see
     that they freely
attack their fathers, and how are they so very different from us?
Except, of course, that they refrain from drafting statutes.

STREPSIADES:

1430   If you're so keen to take after farmyard fowl, why don't you start
     eating chicken shit and roosting on a perch in the henhouse?

PHEIDIPPIDES:

Sir, your analogy is hardly relevant, and I am sure Socrates would
     agree with me.

STREPSIADES:

Then stop hitting me. Otherwise you'll come to regret it.

PHEIDIPPIDES:

And why would that be?

STREPSIADES:

1435   Well, when you have a son of your own,
you'll not have the right to beat him, as I did you!

PHEIDIPPIDES:

But what if I don't have a son? Then I would have suffered
for nothing, and you'll be laughing at me from beyond the grave.

     (Strepsiades addresses the audience.)

STREPSIADES:

You know what, friends, he does have a point, and it seems
only proper that we give the young the benefit of the doubt now
     and again.
I suppose it's only reasonable that we should suffer a little if we step
     out of line.

PHEIDIPPIDES:
And another thing . . .   1440

STREPSIADES:
No! I can't take it anymore!

PHEIDIPPIDES:
Just listen. Perhaps it will make your suffering seem not so bad.

STREPSIADES:
What are you talking about? Nothing could comfort my pain.

PHEIDIPPIDES:
I shall beat Mother just as I beat you.

STREPSIADES:
WHAT! What are you saying? This is going from bad to worse!

PHEIDIPPIDES:
But I can use the Inferior Argument to defeat you on this very
    subject.   1445
I can prove that it is right to beat one's mother.

STREPSIADES:
And what then?
What then? I ask you!
You're all doomed!
You're going to throw yourself into the abyss.   1450
You, Socrates, and that damned Inferior Argument!

(Strepsiades looks up and calls out.)

Clouds! This is all your fault, you're responsible!
I trusted you, I believed in you!

CHORUS:
You brought this trouble on yourself when you took
the twisting path of wickedness and deceit.   1455

STREPSIADES:
But why didn't you tell me that in the first place?
I'm just a simple old yokel. You lured me into this mess!

CHORUS:
But we always do this.
When we discover a mortal who becomes

1460 enamored by vice, we drive them to despair.
That is how we teach man to have proper respect for the gods.

STREPSIADES:
Oh, Clouds, you've treated me harshly, but you're right,
I should never have tried to get of out paying my debts.

(To Pheidippides.)

Come on, my lad, let's get even with Socrates and Chaerephon,
1465 those villains, it's high time they met their makers!
Let's pay them back for the vile way they deceived us.

PHEIDIPPIDES:
But I must not offend my teachers.

STREPSIADES:
Yes, yes, and "we venerate Zeus, protector of fathers."

PHEIDIPPIDES:
Just listen to you, "father Zeus." You're so old fashioned!
1470 Zeus doesn't exist.

STREPSIADES:
Yes, he does.

PHEIDIPPIDES:
No, he doesn't. "Zeus has been overthrown; Basin is king now."

STREPSIADES:
He hasn't been overthrown. I was misled by this basin.

(Indicating the wine basin set on a stand outside the Pondertorium.)

Oh, what a stupid wretch I am, to believe that a piece of clay
pottery could ever be a god!

PHEIDIPPIDES:
I've had enough of you. You can rant and rave to yourself. I'm not
1475 listening.

(Exit Pheidippides.)

STREPSIADES:
Oh, I must have been completely out of my mind,
to think I rejected the gods because Socrates told me to.
Unbelievable! What was I thinking? Dear, dear Hermes,

take pity on me, please be kind, don't destroy me now.
I know I behaved like a raving maniac, but it was all because of
    them   1480
and their philosophical drivel. I need you now. Help me, tell me
    what
can I do to redeem myself. Should I file a lawsuit against them?
What? What can I do?

(Strepsiades suddenly realizes what he must do.)

Yes, that's it, that's exactly right,
I'm not going to fiddle around with lawsuits. No, I'll burn
those babbling bastards out, that's what I'll do! Xanthias! Xanthias! 1485
Come here at once and bring the ladder and an axe!

*(A slave comes running out with a ladder and an axe. He lays the
ladder against the Pondertorium.)*

I want you to climb up onto the roof of the Pondertorium
and do a hatchet job on their roof, and if you care anything
for your poor old master, you'll really bring the house down
on those charlatans. Light up a torch and hand it to me!   1490

(Xanthias hands him a flaming torch.)

Now it's my turn to call in the debts. Those colossal cheats
are going to pay dearly for what they put me through!

*(Strepsiades and Xanthias climb up onto the roof of the Ponderto-
rium.)*

STUDENT:
Oh! Oh!

STREPSIADES:
"Come torch, send on your mighty blaze!"

(Enter a student, who sees Strepsiades on the roof.)

STUDENT 1:
You there! What are you up to?   1495

STREPSIADES:
I'm demonstrating to your rafters the finer points of my axe!

(Enter another student.)

STUDENT 2:
Ahhh! Who set our house on fire?

STREPSIADES:
You should know, you thieves, you lot stole his cloak!

STUDENT 1:
You'll kill us all! Kill us all!

STREPSIADES:
1500   Well at least you're right about that, as long as I don't
get carried away with my axe and come a cropper!

(Enter Socrates.)

SOCRATES:
You up there. Whatever do you think you are doing?

STREPSIADES:
I am "walking the air to look down on the sun!"

(Enter Chaerephon.)

CHAEREPHON:
Ahhh! Help! I'm suffocating!

SOCRATES:
1505   What about me? I'm going up in smoke!

STREPSIADES:
It serves you right for daring to think that you could snub the gods
and spy on the Moon when she's all exposed. Outrageous!
Chase them down. Smash bash and crash them! We'll teach them
a hundred lessons, but most of all never to offend the gods above!

(Exit Strepsiades and Xanthias into the Pondertorium.)

CHORUS:
1510   *And now it's time we closed this play*
We've performed enough for you today!

(Exit the chorus rapidly offstage.)

XENOPHON

Introduction

Xenophon was born in Athens c. 428 B.C.E. and died c. 354. His family, like that of his contemporary Plato, was fairly well off. His oligarchic, pro-Spartan sympathies probably led to his leaving Athens in 401 B.C.E., and to his formal exile soon after. Once out of Athens, he joined Cyrus the Younger in a failed expedition to capture the Persian throne from his brother Artaxerxes. His *Anabasis* chronicles the expedition and his own part in leading the Greek troops back to Greece. After serving briefly as a mercenary in Thrace, Xenophon fought for Sparta for five years (399–394 B.C.E.). Then for the next thirty years or so, he lived with his wife and two sons as a country gentleman under Spartan protection. His exile was repealed in 369 B.C.E., and he returned to Athens in 365, where he remained until his death.

Xenophon was not a philosopher in any interesting sense. He wrote on hunting, horsemanship, estate management, cavalry command, and military history. His Socrates tends to share these interests, rather than the more philosophical ones familiar from Plato. His general intent was to defend Socrates by portraying him as encouraging young men to become gentlemen like Xenophon himself—free from subjection to their own desires or the authority of an employer, mentally and physically self-disciplined, willing to follow their own good sense where applicable and oracles and divinations elsewhere. Unlike Plato's Socrates, who prefers to ask questions rather than answering them, Xenophon's Socrates is full of practical—and somewhat conservative—advice.

In his *Socrates' Defense to the Jury*, Xenophon's goals are self-advertisedly circumscribed. His aim is not to give a full account of Socrates' trial or even a version of his entire speech of defense. Instead, he aims to solve a problem that seems to have troubled many of his predecessors and has continued to trouble readers of Plato's *Apology*. Socrates, they claim, seems to defy the jury and to weaken his defense in the process. Xenophon thinks that they are right, and he cites Hermogenes' account of Socrates' behavior as evidence. He then argues that this defiance should not be seen as weakness, because it is purposeful. Socrates is tired of living and wants to force the jury to sentence him to death. The contrast with Plato's account couldn't be clearer—or more intriguing.

SOCRATES' DEFENSE TO THE JURY

1   I think it's also worth remembering what Socrates thought about his defense and about the end of his life when he was summoned to court. Of course, others have written about this, and all of them have captured his defiant way of speaking, which makes it clear that Socrates really did speak that way. What they don't make clear, though, is that he already believed he would be better off dead, and so they make his defiance seem rather ill considered.

2   However, Hermogenes the son of Hipponicus[1] was a friend of Socrates, and the kind of thing he reports about him shows that his defiance was deliberate. He reports, for example, that when he saw him discussing anything and everything rather than the trial, he said

3 to him, "Socrates, shouldn't you really have been thinking about what you're going to say in your defense as well?" At first, he replied, "You mean you don't think I've spent my whole life getting ready to make my defense?" Then Hermogenes asked, "How do you mean?" "I mean," he said, "that I've gone through life without doing anything wrong, which I believe is the best way of preparing my defense."

4   Hermogenes responded by asking, "Don't you see the Athenian courts often being led astray by a speech and putting people to death when they've done nothing wrong, and just as often setting people free who have done wrong, because their speech made them take pity or flattered them?" "By Zeus, of course I have," Socrates said, "and what's more, I've tried twice now to think about my defense,

5 but my daimonic sign[2] opposed me." "But that's amazing!" Hermogenes said. "Do you really think it's all that amazing," he replied, "that the god[3] too should believe I'd be better off dead now? Don't you realize I wouldn't concede to any human being that he has lived a better life than I have up to now? You see, I've known all along that I've lived my entire life piously and justly—and that's very gratifying. And these traits have not only caused me to admire myself, but I've

---

1. Not much is known about Hermogenes, the brother of Callias (see Plato, *Apology* 20a5). He was a constant companion of Socrates, present at his deathbed (*Phaedo* 59b7–8). He plays an important role in Plato's *Cratylus*.

2. See *Apology* 31c7–d4.

3. Apollo.

found that my friends admire me for them too. But if I grow even 6
older now, I know that I'll have to go through the trials of old age:
my sight will deteriorate, I'll hear less and less, and I'll become slower
to learn and quicker to forget what I do learn. And if I should realize
I'm deteriorating and reproach myself, how would I get any enjoy- 7
ment out of life?

"It may well be, you know," he went on, "that the god, in his
kindness, is letting me leave life not only at the right time, but also in
the easiest way. For if sentence is passed against me now, I'll obviously
be able to come to the end that—in the judgment of those in charge
of the matter—is the easiest for myself, the least trouble for my
friends, and the cause of the deepest grief over the departed. For
whenever someone leaves his friends with no embarrassing or awk-
ward memories, but passes away when his body is still in good health
and his soul still capable of enjoying friendship, how could he fail to
be mourned? The gods were right," he said, "to prevent me from 8
working out a speech, just when we thought I should be looking for
any possible means of acquittal. Because it's obvious that if I had gone
through with this, instead of getting ready to end my life right now, I
would only have been getting ready to die amid the sufferings
brought on by illness or old age—and old age brings together every
manner of hardship and is utterly bereft of consolation. By Zeus, 9
Hermogenes!" he said, "I don't relish that prospect. But as things are,
I think I've been so favored by gods and men that if I overburden the
jurors by revealing this estimate I have of myself, I'll be choosing to
die, instead of preserving my life by begging, which would be to pur-
chase at the price of death a life that's far inferior to it."

Hermogenes said that this was Socrates' frame of mind when he 10
came forward to speak after his opponents had accused him of not
acknowledging the gods the city acknowledged, introducing new
daimonic activities instead and corrupting the young.[4] "Gentlemen," 11
he said, "the first thing I find amazing about Meletus is what evidence
he could ever have had for saying that I don't acknowledge the gods
the city acknowledges. Because anyone who happened to be around
would see me making sacrifices at the state festivals and on the public
altars—and Meletus himself could have seen this too, if he'd wanted
to. And as for introducing *new* daimonic activities, how could I be 12

---

4. See *Apology* 24c1 note.

doing that by saying a divine voice clearly indicates to me what I must do? After all, some men actually use birdcalls as voices of divination, and others use what people chance to say. And will anyone dispute that the sound of thunder is a significant voice or that it is the most portentous omen? And doesn't even the Pythia herself, on her

13 tripod, use her voice to proclaim messages from the god?[5] And then, you know, there's the idea that the god has foreknowledge of the future and prophesies to whomever he wants; and everyone says this and believes it too, in exactly the ways I'm talking about. But while they speak of bird omens, chance sayings, signs, and seers as their prophetic warnings, I call mine a daimonic thing. And I think that in calling it this I'm speaking more truly and more devoutly than those who attribute the power of the gods to birds. Actually, I also have the following proof that I am not falsely attributing things to the god: for I have reported the god's advice to very many of my friends, and I have never yet been shown to be wrong."

14   There was an uproar among the jurors when they heard this. Some of them didn't believe what had been said; others were envious, suspecting that even from the gods he had obtained greater favors than they had. At this Socrates retorted, "Well now, listen to this too, so that those of you who are so inclined may be even more skeptical about how I have been honored by gods. For when Chaerephon once inquired at Delphi about me, Apollo answered before many witnesses that no man was either freer than me, or more just, or more moderate."[6]

15   Since the jurors naturally created an even greater uproar when they heard this latest assertion, Socrates said in response, "But gentlemen! What the god said through the oracle about me was less than what he said about Lycurgus, the Spartan lawgiver.[7] For they say that when he entered the temple, the god announced, 'I am wondering whether to call you a god or a man.' But he didn't compare *me* to a god—even though he did grant me the distinction of far surpassing other men. Even in this case, however, you shouldn't be too quick to take the god

16 at his word, but examine each of the things he said, one by one. Well then, who do you know who's less enslaved by the body's appetites

---

5. See *Apology* 21a6 note.

6. See *Apology* 20e6–21a8 and notes.

7. Lycurgus was traditionally taken to be the founder of the Spartan constitution.

than myself? And who's freer than I, since I take neither gifts nor pay from anyone? And who on earth could you reasonably consider more just than someone who's so well adapted to his circumstances that he has no need of anyone else's possessions? And how could anyone reasonably deny that I am a wise man, since as soon as I could understand speech, I began seeking out and learning whatever good things I 17 could and have never stopped doing so since? And don't you think the proof that I haven't been working in vain is just this: that a lot of the citizens who aspire to virtue, and a lot of the foreigners, choose me, rather than anyone else, to spend their time with? And even though everyone knows I have the least money to give in return, a lot of people still want to give me some kind of gift: what shall we say is the reason for that? Or for the fact that no one demands payment of debts from me—but, on the contrary, many people agree they owe me a 18 debt of gratitude? Or that, during the blockade,[8] while other people took pity on themselves, I was no worse off than when the city was most prosperous? Or that while others acquire expensive luxuries from the market, I get myself greater pleasures than theirs from my own soul, without expense? Now, assuming that no one could convict me of lying in what I've been saying about myself, how could I not now deserve praise from gods and men?

"Despite all that, Meletus, are you saying that I corrupt the young 19 by doing these things? We do know, don't we, what kinds of things corrupt the young; so why don't you say whether you know of anyone who has gone from reverence to impiety because of me, or from modesty to arrogance, or from temperance to extravagance, or from moderate drinking to drunkenness, or from diligence to negligence, or has been overcome by any other base pleasure?"   20

"Well yes, by Zeus, I do!" Meletus replied. "I know that those you influence obey you rather than their parents." "I admit it," Socrates replied, "at least where education's concerned. You see, people know this is a special concern of mine. And when it comes to health, people trust doctors rather than their parents. And in the meetings of the assembly, I'm sure that all the Athenians trust the ones who speak with the most intelligence rather than their own relations. And then, of course, don't you choose as generals, in preference to your fathers and your brothers—and even, by Zeus, to your own selves—whomever you regard as having the best judgment about warfare?"

---

8. Of Athens by Sparta in 405–404 B.C.E. during the Peloponnesian War.

"That's right, Socrates," Meletus said, "because it makes good sense as well as being the established custom."

21   "Well then," Socrates replied, "don't you think it amazing that whereas the best practitioners in other areas of expertise are not only given an appropriate reward, but are also highly esteemed, I myself, who[9] am considered by some to be the best judge about the greatest good for men—I mean, education—that I am, *for this very reason*, indicted by you on a capital charge?"

22   It's obvious, of course, that Socrates said more than this, and so did friends who spoke on his behalf. But I haven't been concerned to relate everything that went on during the trial; rather, I've been content to show two things: first, that Socrates had always held it of the utmost importance to commit no impiety against the gods or give any appearance of injustice toward men; and secondly, that he nonetheless didn't think he should grovel in order to avoid death,
23   but, on the contrary, he actually believed the right time had come for him to die.

But it was when the sentence had been pronounced that it became even clearer he was thinking this way. For, in the first place, when he was ordered to propose a lesser penalty for himself, he would not do so himself, and he would not allow his friends to either, but he even said it would be an admission of guilt. And then, secondly, when his companions wanted to smuggle him away, he would not go along with it, but he even seemed to make fun of them, asking them whether they perhaps knew of some place outside Attica not accessible to death.

24   When at last the verdict was given, Hermogenes reports that Socrates said, "Well, gentlemen, those who coached the witnesses to perjure themselves and give false testimony against me, and those who complied with their instructions, must be conscious of grievous impiety and injustice on their own part. But as for myself, why should I think any less of myself than before I was condemned? After all, it hasn't been in the least proven that I have done any of the things for which I was indicted. For it hasn't been shown that I make sacrifices or swear oaths to any new daimonic beings in place of Zeus, Hera, and the gods of that pantheon; nor has it been shown that I acknowledge
25   other gods. And how on earth could I corrupt the young, by training

---

9. Reading ὅτι with Stephanus.

them in thrift and endurance? Moreover, when it comes to the crimes that do carry the death penalty—sacrilege, burglary, enslavement, high treason—even the prosecutors themselves don't accuse me of committing any of them. So it strikes me as amazing that you can ever have thought what I've done deserves the death penalty.

"Nor should the fact that I'm being put to death unjustly lead me 26 to have a worse opinion of myself in the slightest. I mean, that's a disgrace to those who have sentenced me; it is no disgrace to me. Far from it. Actually, I find consolation in no less a figure than Palamedes,[10] who came to an end quite similar to my own. For even now, he still lays claim to much finer eulogies than Odysseus,[11] who killed him unjustly. And I know posterity will attest—as the past has done—that I've never yet behaved unjustly toward anyone nor done anything at all shameful, and that I benefited the people who conversed with me, by teaching them free of charge anything good that I could."

After saying that, he walked away in a manner very much in keep- 27 ing with what he'd said, since he was extremely cheerful in expression, bearing, and gait. And when he realized his followers were weeping, he said, "What's this? You're weeping, even now? Why, haven't you long known that there has been a death sentence pronounced against me by nature ever since I was born? However, if I perish at a time when good things might still befall me, then obviously that would be painful for me, as well as for those who wish me well. But if I bring my life to an end at a time when hardships are in store, then I think all of you should be happy at my good fortune."

Now, a certain Apollodorus[12] was there, a man who was extremely 28 fond of Socrates but otherwise a bit simpleminded. "But Socrates," he said, "the thing that I find especially hard to bear is seeing you being put to death unjustly." Hermogenes says that Socrates stroked his head and replied with a good-natured laugh, "Apollodorus, my dearest friend, would you prefer to see me being put to death justly instead?"

It's also said that when he saw Anytus[13] there he said, "Well, this 29 man here is proud of himself as if he'd done a great and noble thing.

---

10. See *Apology* 41b2 note.

11. See *Apology* 41c1 note.

12. See *Apology* 34a2–3 note; *Phaedo* 117d3–6.

13. See *Apology* 18b2 note.

He's having me put to death because when I saw that he was deemed worthy of the greatest honors by the city, I said that he shouldn't confine his son's education to tanning hides. The man is so corrupt that he seems not to realize that, of the two of us, the real victor is the one
30 who has achieved what is more beneficial and noble for all time. Furthermore," he went on, "Homer, too, attributes to some of those who are coming to the end of their lives the power to foretell the future; and so I also want to prophesize. You see, I once had some brief acquaintance with Anytus' son, and he didn't strike me as a weak-minded man. So I declare that he will not persevere in that slavish way of life his father has prepared for him; but for want of a good man to take care of him, he'll succumb to some shameful desire and sink deep into depravity."

31   What he said was right. The youth took to wine, couldn't stop drinking day or night, and ended up utterly worthless to his city, his friends, and himself. So Anytus, even though dead, also acquired a bad reputation, due to the bad upbringing he gave his son and his own bad judgment.

32   Socrates, by singing his own praises in court, then, brought the resentment of the jurors down upon himself and forced them to condemn him all the more. To my mind, however, he met with the fate of those who are loved by the gods. I mean, he escaped the most irk-
33 some part of life and had the easiest of deaths. And he demonstrated the strength of his character: when he realized it was better for him to die than to carry on living, he showed no weakness in the face of death—any more than he turned his back on any other good thing—but accepted it, and went to meet it, in good spirits.

34   As for myself, knowing as I do the man's wisdom and nobility of character, it's impossible for me to forget him or to remember him without praising him. And if anyone who seeks virtue has met with any more beneficial companion than Socrates, I consider him worthy of being called the most blessed of all.

Further Reading

Background

Beck, F. A. G. *Greek Education 450–350 B.C.* London: Methuen, 1964.

Burkert, W. *Greek Religion.* Cambridge, Mass.: Harvard University Press, 1985.

Dover, K. J. *Greek Homosexuality.* Cambridge, Mass.: Harvard University Press, 1978.

Hornblower, S., and A. Spawforth. *The Oxford Classical Dictionary.* 3rd ed. Oxford: Oxford University Press, 1996.

Irwin, T. H. *Classical Thought.* Oxford: Oxford University Press, 1989.

Joint Association of Classical Teachers. *The World of Athens: An Introduction to Classical Athenian Culture.* Cambridge: Cambridge University Press, 1984.

MacDowell, D. M. *The Law in Classical Athens.* Ithaca: Cornell University Press, 1978.

Plato and His Socrates

Benson, H. H., ed. *Essays on the Philosophy of Socrates.* New York: Oxford University Press, 1992.

Brickhouse, T. C., and N. D. Smith. *The Philosophy of Socrates.* Boulder: Westview Press, 2000.

De Strycker, E., and S. R. Slings. *Plato's Apology of Socrates.* Leiden: Brill, 1994.

Grote, G. *Plato and the Other Companions of Socrates.* Vols. 1–3. London: John Murray, 1865.

Irwin, T. H. *Plato's Ethics.* New York: Oxford University Press, 1995.

Kahn, C. H. *Plato and the Socratic Dialogue.* Cambridge: Cambridge University Press, 1996.

McPherran, M. L. *The Religion of Socrates.* University Park: Penn State Press, 1996.

Reeve, C. D. C. *Socrates in the Apology: An Essay on Plato's Apology of Socrates.* Indianapolis: Hackett, 1989.

Vlastos, G. *Socrates: Ironist and Moral Philosopher.* Cambridge: Cambridge University Press, 1991.

Aristophanes

Dover, K. J. *Aristophanes: Clouds.* Oxford: Clarendon Press, 1968.

———. *Aristophanic Comedy.* Berkeley: University of California Press, 1972.

Xenophon

Cooper, J. M. "Notes on Xenophon's Socrates." In *Reason and Emotion: Essays on Ancient Moral Psychology and Ethical Theory.* Princeton: Princeton University Press, 1999.

Morrison, D. "On Professor Vlastos' Xenophon." *Ancient Philosophy* 7 (1987): 9–22.

———. "Xenophon's Socrates on the Just and the Lawful." *Ancient Philosophy* 15 (1995): 329–347.

Tredennick, H., and R. Waterfield. *Xenophon: Conversations of Socrates.* Harmondsworth: Penguin, 1990.

Vander Waerdt, Paul. *The Socratic Movement.* Ithaca: Cornell University Press, 1994.